Facing Nadal
Symposium of a Champion

By Scoop Malinowski

ISBN-13: 978-1508825715

ISBN-10: 1508825718

I will never forget the first time seeing Rafael Nadal play. It was at the US Open in 2003, a second round match on Grandstand in late afternoon vs. Younes El Aynaoui. At the time, Nadal was seventeen years old and ranked no. 45 in the world. The "Rockin' Moroccan" was the no. 21 seed.

Nadal had won his first round match against veteran countryman Fernando Vicente, ranked no. 61 in the world, in routine fashion: 6-4 6-3 6-3.

Nadal was a tennis tornado against El ynaoui, playing with a furious ferocity, beyond anything the sport had ever witnessed. Lleyton Hewitt's tenacious intensity was the previous benchmark, but this   young raging bull's burning desire was a different level. He played with a drive & determination so strong, it was almost as if his career was at stake.

I can still remember details of this match over a decade ago like it was last week. Nadal challenged El Aynaoui and pushed him to the limits. Down an early break, Nadal fought back to level it, and then forced a first set tiebreaker. The jam-packed Grandstand was in pandemonium because of this kid's fight back qualities.

Again, Nadal was down the mini break but, again he leveled it, before finally losing the tiebreaker, 8-6. During the frenzied atmosphere of the first set, evoked by Nadal's fighting spirit, I curiously looked over to the Nadal box about twenty yards to my right, expecting to see his uncle, agent and others jumping out of their seats in excitement and joy. But they were all completely stoic. As if this is exactly what they expected to happen, as if they had already seen this same drama a hundred times before.

Nadal ended up losing the match 67 36 67 but it became obvious right then in that first set that this kid was going to make it big. Nothing in the world was going to deny or defy this kid's quest to be the best.

The rest is history. Clay court king. Hard court champion. Wimbledon champion. Davis Cup titan. Number one in the world. Global icon. Impeccably mannered sportsman, hero of children and adults all over the world.

Watching this remarkable world champion on TV and live at an ATP World Tour event, from an outsider's perspective, is an unforgettable experience. For this book, the latest edition of my "Facing..." series, I've pursued a different point of view of Rafa - from the ATP players who have actually competed on a court against Nadal. Over 55 players have shared their detailed memories, observations, and anecdotes of playing tennis with Rafael Nadal, their matches, practices, and just being with him on the Tour.

So many different people helped make this book possible: all the players who graciously shared their time and thoughts, the ATP Tour and tournament officials who helped to get this arduous task completed. And finally, the exceptional photography of my friend Henk Abbink, one of the best in the business.

I hope you enjoy this book about one of the most unique and exciting champions in the history of sport...

Mark "Scoop" Malinowski
Bradenton, Florida
April 2015

Facing Nadal

By Scoop Malinowski

Table of Contents

Chapter 1: Media and Insider Perspectives of Rafa

(Photo by Gail Koskorelos.)

Jimmy Connors on meeting Rafa for the first time:

Scoop: Where did you meet Nadal?

Jimmy Connors: "Nadal — we saw him during the Palm Springs event. Very, very shy…very…he's a very interesting young man. Very strong. It was interesting for me just to see somebody 18 - 19-years-old with a build like that, that goes out and takes that to the tennis court. And shows his athleticism when he plays. But very shy, very reserved, laid back. Almost nervous to be around, and be a part of it. But very interesting."

Scoop: A guy like you must appreciate his intensity levels. What do you think of his intensity?

Jimmy Connors: "Oh, I like it [smiles]. I wish a lot more of that would be around. To show what you're feeling and your abilities and the way you go about trying to use your abilities. His passion and his emotion and what he's trying to get across to the crowd — that's what it's all about, in my opinion [smiles]."

Yevgeny Kafelnikov: "Nadal is the person I like to watch the most besides of course Safin."

Question: Why Rafa?

Yevgeny Kafelnikov: "Well, I think he's a character, he brings charisma to the courts. He's got good, fresh energy."

"He's like one of those self-made millionaires."

Luke Jensen in 2011: "My favorite player to watch...number one, to be perfectly honest, I could watch Rafael Nadal practice, I could watch him in the players' lounge, the man is so intense. And so focused and has so much purpose and drive that he's truly such an overachiever because he doesn't have the biggest guns, he doesn't have the most talent. This is all self-made. He's like one of those self-made millionaires. Came from nothing really. Plays with his opposite hand. He's not left-handed, he's right-handed. He's not a hard court player but he became one. He's not a grass court player, he became on. He's evolved. How many players, that we've covered now, they get to a point and it is too hard and they don't evolve. And they just kinda sit in the same spot. And they drop and they come back – and this guy continues to get better. His new challenge is Djokovic, truly is, another kind of chapter in his life where he's gonna figure it out, it may be the next tournament, it may be next year, I don't know, but the guy is not going away. And I have so much respect for that attitude."

Gustavo Kuerten discusses in 2007 what it would be like to play his best tennis against Nadal's best tennis in a hypothetical French Open final:

"I don't know, anything can happen [smiles]. I think it would be very interesting. I think a lot of people would like to solve that question [smiles]."

Question: Do you study him, watch his matches in Paris thinking if you could beat him?

Gustavo Kuerten: "I think it's not the way to think like that. I think he's getting better and better still, every year I watch him play on any surface, he's still improving. And he has already a big gap between the other players. So that's really taking a lot of attention for myself. I wouldn't believe he would get so much distance from the other players."

Question: Who are some of your favorite ATP players to watch?

Gustavo Kuerten: "I like watching many of the players. There's not any one that I prefer the most but I think the characters left still are Safin, Haas, besides Federer, Nadal, Djokovic, Roddick - probably the ones that, for me, bring more attention from the crowd."

James Blake: "My first impression of Rafa then was he was a clay-courter playing on hard courts. He was playing with a lot of topspin, hitting the ball heavy, but not attacking the ball, not moving forward at all. He sort of counted on his defense and his movement to win a lot of matches. He did it exceptionally well, obviously.

"I also remember specifically, I had never even hit with him before I played him, the first couple balls in warm-up, he hit the ball so heavy, I actually thought I was in trouble from the start. Once the match started, he was hitting the ball shorter and playing with a lot of margin and not being as aggressive. As I've seen him now and practiced with him much more recently, that guy is gone. He's so much more effective with being aggressive, with taking his game and imposing it on me, like I said, being more effective with his serve. He's still one of the best movers, moves so well side to side."

(Quotes from Richard Pagliaro.)

Pete Sampras: "Quite honestly I don't think he really needs to (break the Grand Slam record). He's won all the majors, he's won the Olympics and he's dominated his main rival in Roger, and I don't think his goal (is to win) 16, 17 or 18. I think his goal is to improve as a tennis player and if it happens great. He could do it. You look at what's ahead -- it's a lot of work. He's got to work so hard for every match that he plays. But he's a beast. The kid is relentless."

John McEnroe in 2007:   It's really tough to play this guy. I watch this guy play every time I come here for this tournament (in Rome). This guy is unbelievable on this surface. He's one of the best -- he's like the

Borg of this era. Borg was incredibly fit and fast and you didn't win any free points against him. He just had this mental edge. In those days when guys used wood racquets, it wasn't as if you could get the ball by him. His is like a different style. Same sort of end result. Just seems like he's unbeatable. I just can't see the guy losing. But having said that, yesterday he looked vulnerable. I mean, he could have lost that match. So that's -- I think that's a reason for hope for some of these other guys. (Nikolay) Davydenko definitely had him, just didn't look comfortable for whatever reason. I think some of it just caught up with him a little bit, even for him physically. I think he's going take a couple weeks and he'll be a lot fresher again. He'll be -- it's going to be pretty tough to beat the guy. I mean, I'd like to see that: Some guy beating him, just to see how that could be done.

Q. He's playing a lot doubles, which is something that you used to do, probably to improve his volley, yeah?

JOHN McENROE: Well, the irony, at least to me, is that to me he's serving and staying back. So it's like -- I mean, I guess a couple times he's come in, but for the most part it looks like he's practicing for singles instead of working on parts of his game that he may need to improve, because that's what most guys do. Okay, I'll play some doubles so I can work on my volley or the return. He's not doing that. He's just out there continuing to do what he does. So it's like, Why in the world does he need to do that? I'm sure that it's not easy for some of the guys that he plays, but to me if he's going to play doubles he should try to do --

because his serve and his volley have improved. He's got some pretty good hands. He's got some -- you know, he volleys pretty well. His serve has gotten some more pop and he's gotten better there. So it seems like there's no reason why he shouldn't, if he's going to play doubles, do that. But I don't know.

Q. Do you think there's a danger in playing doubles, because you did that, rather than practice? That he's over-extending himself?

JOHN McENROE: Well, I think he did yesterday. I think he felt that a little bit. So I think even -- I was sitting next to (Carlos) Moya during the Djokovic match and he was saying, I mean, Look you don't need to play this match. Don't worry about it, or whatever. (Rafa replied) No, no, no, I want to play. Like he's really eager to play. And (Moya) was like, You are? He was sort of surprised at how into it he is. So it's unbelievable in a way. But I think they're just going to really tell him like, Look you're not playing doubles, and as a matter of fact -- I mean, I don't know what's going to happen. I don't want to be the reason that he -- but I could definitely see where he's got more than enough to be ready to play in Paris already, and he doesn't want to lose to anybody. He's that type of guy. He's going to go there and try to win it. So I don't know they may be. We don't have long to wait.

Corinne Debreuil (Photographer from France): "Nadal is the most photogenic guy for me. Each time you make a picture it's a good one. And he's very expressive. You can expect a lot from him. Especially when he wins. Great celebrations. And the stretching a lot, sometimes it makes really good pictures. For me, this is the greatest and most expressive guy to take pictures of. For me, the best one - him and Serena (Williams). (Wow.) Yeah, really. Every shot can be a good one or a very good one."

Georges Homsi (French journalist): "He's the most genuinely humble player or champion of his rank. That strikes me most of all with Nadal. We have a lot of players that are... Federer is extremely nice, extremely friendly, but I find him to be... I think that was the way he (Nadal) was educated. He was taught to be humble and that's good education and that really shows. That's the first thing that comes to mind when I think of Nadal."

Question: Any examples of these qualities by Rafa?

Georges Homsi: "Win or lose, the way he analyzes. You can feel whether somebody is really sincere or whether somebody is saying it to look good. He sincerely is the total opposite of arrogance. And the contrast is how fierce he is on the court. More than anyone I've ever seen. And that makes a nice combination. An exceptional human being/champion."

Question: Lasting memory or anecdote of Rafa on or off court?

Georges Homsi: "I only interviewed him once on-on-one in Mallorca and that was a nice moment. I can't give you that as an example of what I was saying. More day in and day out, having seen him around on the Tour and the media, around the people.
A really good guy. And also, he keeps track of other players. Even players have told me how they win the small tournament and he congratulates them, a 250 event, when he's won seven slams. The players said he said 'congratulations for two months ago because I haven't seen you since then.' He keeps that in mind and he really means it. So he's a guy I really appreciate."

Question: How do you feel the media generally feels towards Rafa? Similar to you?

Georges Homsi: "I don't know. I can't speak for others. I wouldn't see a reason why not. But he always has people who don't like him. You know, is his style of game my favorite? No. I prefer to watch Federer. You always find people who are pro-Federer and pro-Nadal. It's silly, in my opinion. Both are extremely great ambassadors for the game."

Akatsuki Uchida (Japanese Journalist): "I remember one of my colleagues went to the players lounge and he said he saw Rafa. He was quite shy. He was still seventeen at the time. He wasn't hanging around other players and he looked really shy. So at the time my colleague didn't realize it was Nadal. And then he went on the court and he behaved very passionate and aggressive. So he said he was quite impressed by how he changes on the court."

Question: Like Clark Kent to Superman?

Akatsuki Uchida: "Yeah [smiles]. That's right."

Boxing Champion **Sergio Martinez** calls Nadal his most admired person:

By Scoop Malinowski

This interview with the champion boxer Sergio "Maravilla" Martinez offered an unexpected insight about Rafael Nadal...

Sergio Martinez is the current WBC Middleweight champion of the world and was in New York on Thursday for a press conference to promote his November 20 title defense against Paul "The Punisher" Williams in Atlantic City, NJ.

Typical for a Biofile, I asked Martinez, who was born in Argentina and now lives in Oxnard, CA, what are the people qualities he most admires?

Through the interpreter he stated, "The guy from the tennis – Rafa Nadal."

Why him, I asked, for some elaboration.

"Because he's great. You need to meet him to know how great he is. He's a great person."

Thinking that Martinez met Nadal, I asked where did they meet?

"I had the pleasure to shake hands with him at the tournament in Madrid, that's all," said the polite and classy 35-year-old gladiator, who turned pro in Argentina in 1997 and has a ring record of 45-2-2 (24 KO's). "I did not meet him personally, I know him from that side, like a fan, not like a person or a friend. He was one of many that I shake hands and it was a great moment for me. But I only know him from that side as a fan, not as a personal friend."

I then asked Sergio if he was aware if Nadal knew that he was a world champion boxer?

"No, no, absolutely not."

Placido Domingo on Tennis

I did this interview with the famous tenor in Arthur Ashe Stadium at the US Open in 2009.

Question: How did you become introduced to tennis?

Placido Domingo: "Oh. Years and years back. I have been following since the days of Jimmy Connors and Ilie Nastase. Eventhough it was before I understood the sport. But I start with it, I like very much the way they play. Then I follow very much Bjorn Borg, Guillermo Vilas, then Ivan Lendl, then of course Boris Becker. Finally, Pete Sampras, who I was very much a big, big fan of Sampras. I followed most of his career. Now I follow very much what Federer does. Even though it was very hard to say he will pass Sampras - but, you know, I think it has to happen. Now it has been Nadal playing. I'm Spanish, I really love his playing. I hope that one day he will be there fighting for some more Grand Slams, just like Federer has done. And I think that, at the moment, it's a very difficult situation, because there are four, five, six players, that, at any moment, can get really deep - either Federer or Nadal. I like to see Nadal win."

Question: What is the appeal of tennis? Why do you love it?

Placido Domingo: "I think it's such an elegant sport. It's exciting. So personal, you know? So personal. Really, you have to develop the strength, you have to have all the skills. You just have to know the other players, to follow very much what they do. So you have to study completely. It's just like...you never end it. Because new players are always coming. And it's not like you know everything. And you have to constantly adapt and you have to play according against who you are playing. And so this is a very exciting thing, especially if you are not somebody who can serve twenty, twenty-five, thirty aces in a match. So then you have to know very much the rival. Because if you have a lot of aces, sometimes you can win with the service. It's not so easy if you don't have a service and he's very, very powerful. So it becomes more difficult."

Question: Most memorable match you remember?

Placido Domingo: "Well, I have to say I saw some of the matches between Agassi and Sampras in Wimbledon and here (US Open). And certainly the last two matches between Nadal and Federer in Wimbledon. And this year between Federer and Nadal was really phenomenal, phenomenal match. I love the ladies also. The tennis, I think, is also so exciting. I think one of the most exciting games I saw was between Billie Jean King and the Australian girl (Evonne) Goolagong. So that was really quite a game. But it's exciting. I follow tennis all my life. We were in Lima, Peru the day before yesterday. I saw, myself, with some friends, we were watching the (R16) game of Nadal with (Gael) Monfils."

Question: Which tournaments have you been to?

Placido Domingo: "I have been at Wimbledon and Roland Garros. At Wimbledon, I saw on many occasions, Sampras, I saw Lendl, I saw Boris Becker. In the French Open, I saw Federer. I saw Nadal this last year. Actually, this is my first US Open tonight. I hope we can see more matches here."

The Biofile Rafael Nadal

(This is an Interview I did with then little-known, seventeen-year-old Nadal at the outdoor player lounge area at the 2003 U.S. Open around eight at night. Rafa and his team were leaving the grounds at transportation. I asked to do this interview for a couple of minutes, Uncle Toni and agent Carlos Costa let us talk, without a translator or monitor, about 30 yards away in the picnic area as they waited in the parking lot for their car. Nadal's English was good enough to complete the interview...)

Ht: 6-1 Wt: 188

DOB: June 3, 1986 In: Manacor, Mallorca, Spain.

Childhood Heroes: "I don't know. I don't have."

Hobbies/Interests: "I like fishing. I like (to) stay with my friends. Go to beach. Go to cinema."

Favorite Movies: "Gladiator, Titanic."

Musical Tastes: "Bryan Adams, Mana — he's Mexican."

Early Tennis Memory: "Four hours — practice one or two times a week."

Favorite Meal: "Fish."

Favorite Breakfast Cereal: "Frosted Flakes mixed with hot chocolate."

Favorite Ice Cream Flavor: "Vanilla."

Pre-Match Feeling: "Play with incredible motivation. A little bit nervous, but good."

First Job: "Tennis."

Greatest Sports Moment: "I don't know. I have a lot of good moments. When I was young I won the World Cup. Federer in Miami. I won my first ATP title two weeks before (in Sopot, Poland). That's good."

Most Painful Moment: "I don't know. When I stay injured three months (stress fracture in left ankle joint in 2004). Missed Monte Carlo, Rome, Hamburg, Paris (Roland Garros), Wimbledon."

Closest Tennis Friends: "I have all the Spanish players. And I have good relations with all players. Carlos Moya. I know him for so long. I know him very well. He's very sharp. He's a great person even outside the game of tennis. A great guy. One of the best players in the world. I get along very well with Carlos."

Funniest Players Encountered: "I don't know."

Toughest Competitors: "Competitors...all the players, they are playing good. And I think the best player now is Federer. But all players good. Hewitt is playing very well now."

Favorite Tournament(s): "I like many of them. I cannot name just one."

Childhood Dream: "I like a lot the futbol, the soccer. But I like my first dream is any one day I can do the No. 1 in tennis."

Favorite Athletes To Watch: "Ronaldo. Thierry Henry. Frank Lampard. Zidane. Ronaldino. Pau Gasol — he's playing in Memphis. (Tennis?) Federer — he plays very nice. He can do all the shots. I like him. And Hewitt. Because I like the mentality."

Favorite Vacation Spot: "In Mallorca."

Funny Tennis Memory: "Hmmm. I don't know because I have a lot moments funny and a lot of moments good."

People Qualities Most Admired: "For me, is good. The good persons."

Chapter 2:   Facing Rafa Interviews

(Artwork by Andres Bella.)

(Photo by Ziggy.)

Players discuss memories of what it's like to compete against Rafael Nadal on the tennis court...

"I didn't realize he played so well, I wouldn't have been so nice to him [laughs]."

Pat Cash: "I played Nadal when he was a few weeks from being fifteen. In Mallorca. Boris Becker pulled out of the senior match and so they asked me last minute to come in and play, and play the world junior champion. And I said, 'Yeah sure. I don't mind playing. The show must go on.'   A bit of entertainment. I got a great photo of him, actually of us together.   He played the same way. Obviously, he didn't hit the ball as hard then. But he played the same intensity, top spin. I was kind of shocked by it all [smiles]."

"As a young kid his age, it wasn't as if it was something I couldn't handle but, I mean, the crowd was quite amused when he won the first set against me. And I was sort of being nice to him, Okay, no more Mister Nice Guy. Because this kid is really good. He'll beat me if he can. It's not sort of like a fun game. He won the first set and the crowd thought it was hilarious. They were roaring for us. So we were on the court together, so I started chip-charging, serve and volley, that sort of stuff, won the second set pretty comfortably - 6-2 I think. The ten-point tiebreaker. As I said before, 99% of the kids would have choked. And fallen apart. And he was just tearing everywhere. All over the court. And hit some unbelievable winners. And you now, then I was 38, I was still hitting the ball pretty well."

"And so I lost that match. I don't remember what the

score was. It was close. He didn't get nervous or anything. Obviously, he didn't have anything to lose. But I came in the locker room after, the guys sort of looked at me, just to look at my reaction. And my reaction was losing to a fourteen year old. And I just sort of looked at them, Wow, this kid is something else. "Yeah, yeah, yeah,' the players said. I actually played pretty well. And they just sort of looked at me, like, Oh God, how embarrassing is that? And so I kept it pretty quiet for a couple of years. When he won his first French Open, I told the story [smiles]. When he won his second French Open, I told the story a bit more. But yeah, it was clear to me, because I had a tennis academy, so I saw a lot of juniors come through, top juniors in Australia, in the world, and he was something else. Something special."

Question: Have you crossed paths with Nadal since that match over a decade ago?

Pat Cash: "Yeah, yeah, plenty of times. Yeah, I tell the story and we have a bit of a laugh about it. I suppose I can say I lost to the greatest clay court player on clay, even though he was a teenager at the time [smiles]. He won a couple of French Opens when he was still a teenager. So it wasn't a real disgrace to lose to him, even though he was very young."

Question: Such a nice, humble kid, wasn't he?

Pat Cash: "Yeah, he was. He didn't really speak any English then. I believe his uncle was there with him. Before the match I was sort of looking out for him, 'Hey, we're gonna have fun, it's okay, relax.' I didn't realize he played so well. I wouldn't have been so nice to him [laughs]. But yeah, he is a very humble kid. And very polite. Exceptionally polite. I was sitting late last year with Mats Wilander, sort of sitting in on Nadal's press conference, in Basel. We were sitting in the back there. He came - went to leave - then he spotted us. He walked over at the press conference to shake hands with us. It was just a quick hello but it was quite special. Mats and I both commented, 'I don't think any other player would have done that.' He's very polite and respectful. It's very nice to see."

"The moment came to me."

Lukas Rosol: "The best I ever felt on court...second round Wimbledon against Rafa 2012. I wish it was like this more times. I felt really good. I felt pretty comfortable. Everything I touched was going in pretty well."

Question: When did you get the feeling you were going to win the match?

Lukas Rosol: "There was no feeling. I just played my game. I just concentrate on myself. And the moment came to me."

Nadal leads series 2-1

2012 Wimbledon Grass R64 Rosol 6-7, 6-4, 6-4, 2-6, 6-4
2014 Doha   Hard R32 Nadal 6-2, 7-6
2014 Wimbledon Grass R64 Nadal 4-6, 7-6, 6-4, 6-4

"I had a fantastic match, hitting 50 winners, I still lost in the end."

Gilles Simon

Question: Memories of your great match with Nadal?

Gilles Simon: "Where? Here (US Open) against Rafa? Which one? Indian Wells?

Scoop: Madrid.

Gilles Simon: "I beat him in Madrid. But I had a nice one with him in Rome, even if I lost it. So the one in Madrid. I would say three good memories of the matches with Rafa. The one I won of course 2008 in Madrid when Rafa played his incredible year, winning Wimbledon for the first time, the French of course for the fourth time, winning the Olympics, becoming number one. Playing at home with support of his home crowd. It was like a really nice feeling to be there. The atmosphere was one of the best that I ever had on a tennis court, even if they were all cheering for him. It was a very good performance to beat him there. I had a fantastic match I played this year in Rome on the clay, hitting 50 winners, I mean I played one of the best matches I ever played, even if I still lost in the end. But it was fun and it was very important for me to see that I was still able to give him some trouble on a good day and that I think he remembers this match."

"And the last one is a special one I played here. The match was nothing special, the year he won the tournament he was playing good. I lost 64 64 61 but I had my son (Timothe) two days before I played against him. And I just played this match really relaxed. I said, Okay if I lose, it's fine, I'm gonna go home and see my baby. And if I win, it's always great to beat Rafa. And I was on the center court with no pressure at all. And it was a nice feeling to be there just trying to play, a nice feeling."

Question: Rafa seems to bring out the best in you for some reason?

Gilles Simon: "Yeah, because to play Rafa is really demanding. Physically and mentally and he's one of these guys when you are scared, that if you don't do a good job, you will maybe lose one-zero-one because he's not going to give you anything. When you prepare for Rafa you really need to be ready for the worst. And finally it's pushing you to do your best, to hit good, to be focused on every point. And that's why I played many great matches with him."

Nadal leads series 7-1

2006   Marseilles   Hard   R16   Nadal   7-5, 6-4

2008   Australian Open   Hard   R32   Nadal 7-5, 6-2, 6-3

2008   Madrid Masters Hard   SF   Simon   3-6, 7-5, 7-6 (6)

2009   Australian Open   Hard QF   Nadal   6-2, 7-5, 7-5

2010   US Open   Hard R32   Nadal   6-4, 6-4, 6-2

2012   Monte Carlo Masters   Clay   SF   Nadal   6-3, 6-4

2014   Rome Masters   Clay   R32   Nadal 7-6, 6-7, 6-2

2015   Indian Wells Masters Hard   R16   Nadal   6-2, 6-4

"One of the biggest challenges in, not only tennis, but in all sport."

Dominic Thiem: "I faced him in Paris where obviously he lost one match in his career. It was maybe...it's one of the biggest challenges in, not only tennis, but in all sport...to face Rafa in Paris. But it was a good experience for me and I think it helped me a lot."

Question: Did anything surprise you about being on the court with him live, instead of seeing him on TV or from the side?

Dominic Thiem: "It was completely new. It was my first year last year on the Tour and I new everything, everybody only from the TV. And then all of a sudden I was matched in Paris against the nine-time champion. So it was a very good experience and also helpful."

Question: What did you learn that day?

Dominic Thiem: "That I still (have) a long way to go [smiles]."

Nadal leads series 1-0

2014 Roland Garros   Clay   R64   Nadal   6-2, 6-2, 6-3

"He beat me always."

Marcel Granollers: "I played him a lot. As a kid and on ATP. Everyone knows him, how big his game is as a player to play against him is very difficult. He's pushing so much pressure on you when he play with his forehand. And he's a big fighter so it's tough to play against him."

Question: Most memorable match you had with Rafa?

Marcel Granollers: "The best match that I play against him was two years ago in Paris Bercy. I lost 57 57. I would say I was much closer to win one set."

Question: What is your first memory of Rafa?

Marcel Granollers: "First memory is when we play under 12, because we are the same age. So we play under 12 in Spanish Championship in Segovia near Madrid. So since we are very young we play a lot together. Representing Spain in under 12 and under 14, under 16. So we have a lot of moments together. It's nice to see him, how well he plays."

Question: What details do you remember about that first match with Rafa when you were twelve?

Marcel Granollers: "He beat me always [laughs]. So since he was very young he was a very good competitor. Very good fighter. He had something special and now he can play big moment, big stadium, big finals, so I'm happy for him."

Question: As you know him for so long, how has Rafa's game changed over many years?

Marcel Granollers: "Of course, he improved a lot. He improved his serve, his backhand now is very good, very solid. And when he's playing good he's very aggressive with the forehand. So I think he was improving every year."

Question: Lasting memory or anecdote of Rafa?

Marcel Granollers: "He's a very nice guy. When you need something, when you ask him to autograph my t-shirt for a friend of mine or picture with a friend of mine and he's always open minded to do it."

Nadal leads series 3-0

2012 Indian Wells Masters   Hard   R32   Nadal 6-1, 6-4

2012 Rome Masters   Clay   R16   Nadal 6-1, 6-1

2013 Paris Masters   Hard   R32   Nadal 7-5, 7-5

"He's a really nice guy."

Ivo Karlovic: "Well, with me, because I know I'm going to win most of my service games, so it's not all that different between playing him and any other player out there. Because an ace is an ace against anybody. So it isn't really any different. He's really quick. He passes well. And from the baseline I didn't feel he's hitting unbelievable. There is not a lot of busy points from him."

Question: Most memorable match with Rafa?

Ivo Karlovic: "It was in Indian Wells maybe 2011 quarterfinal. It was real difficult match. I had opportunities then in the end I lost 76 in the third set. So that was the most memorable for me."

Question: Is he the hardest for you to play?

Ivo Karlovic: "Again, with me it's different from...like

me and Isner against anybody is pretty much the same. It's all about our serves and how we're gonna do in the crucial points. So if he's more difficult I don't know."

Question: Lasting memory or Rafa, on or off court?

Ivo Karlovic: "I mean, he's a really nice guy off the court. Nothing that I can remember. But he's a really nice guy."

Nadal lead series 4-0

2004   Milan   Carpet   R32   Nadal   7-5, 6-7, 6-1

2008   Queens Club   Grass QF   Nadal 6-7, 7-6 7-6 (4)

2010   Australian Open   Hard R16   Nadal   6-4, 4-6, 6-4, 6-4

2011   Indian Wells Masters   Hard   QF Nadal   5-7, 6-1, 7-6 (7)

"Speaking with Rafa you feel that he is nice."

Ricardas Berankis: "I never played with him, just practice together. He's a great guy. Rafa is a very nice guy. There's really not much to say because he's a great guy."

Question: Did anything surprise you about being on the court with him for the first time?

Ricardas Berankis: "Of course, his intensity. And focus. On every like...not even every point but every shot he makes is quite incredible. And everybody should learn from him, his focus and dedication."

Question: Where did you hit together with Rafa?

Ricardas Berankis: "A few tournaments here and there. I don't remember."

Question: Lasting memory or anecdote of Rafa on or off court?

Ricardas Berankis: "He's a nice person. Sometimes you speak with a person, you see maybe the person is not nice. But you speak with Rafa and you feel it, that he is nice."

"He's not going to stop until he can destroy you."

Sergiy Stakhovsky: "There was one match I had with Nadal, it was in Davis Cup and he killed me. Not much I can remember from that, I lost love, love and four on clay in Madrid. And that wasn't my best memory."

Question: Is it enjoyable to play Rafa or is it too challenging to enjoy?

Sergiy Stakhovsky: "It's hard. It's hard because he's going after every shot. And he's going to stay with you as long as it takes and he's not going to stop until he can destroy you. And I got the feeling after 60 60 that he's not going to stop until he's gonna give me three bagels. But I managed to fight him off."

Question: Lasting memory of Rafa on or off court?

Sergiy Stakhovsky: "The last time I saw him was at Wimbledon. He's a normal person in the locker room. That's where I see him. I don't see him off the court much. On the court he's confident, concentrated and motivated. As any of us. No less, no more."

Nadal leads series 1-0

2013   Davis Cup World Group Play-Off   Clay   Nadal 6-0, 6-0, 6-4

"It was unbelievable change in the Madrid match."

Fernando Verdasco

Question: Memories of your big win vs. Nadal in Madrid?

Fernando Verdasco: "The memories are great. My first victory as a professional against Rafa. It took my best play as possible to beat him. Against a player like him, losing so many times and winning in Madrid, my hometown, with all my family and friends in front of me...it was like impossible to be better than that."

Question: You came close many times...

Fernando Verdasco: "Yeah many times [smiles]."

Question: Did you do anything different in Madrid? What was it that finally got you over the hump?

Fernando Verdasco: "I don't even know [smiles]. I think I was even laughing because it was one of the times that I wasn't even close to winning. I was 5-2 down in the third. He was serving, then all of a sudden, everything changed so quick. It went from 5-2 on his serve and I won 7-5. So it was like unbelievable change in that match. And many times I had like a break up in the third or like match point and I finally lost. So I don't even know why [smiles]."

Question: Is Rafa the hardest guy for you to play?

Fernando Verdasco: "With Roger, he's also a tough guy because I never beat him. I played with him like much less time than with Rafa. With Rafa, I think we played like fourteen times and I only beat him once as a professional. I think me and Roger only played four. So it's a big difference. And then I beat Murray and I beat Djokovic. I think Rafa and Roger are the toughest. But all these four players are like really tough to play and to beat."

***

Press conference by Verdasco after he defeated Nadal in three sets at Miami Open on March 29, 2015:

Question. After the second set, what was going through your mind? Because you had played well the first set, and then you lost two breaks in a row. You were broken twice to lose the second set.

FERNANDO VERDASCO: Yeah, well, what I said on the court right after the match, no? They asked me the same. I said that I was just trying to think about how the first set, how I played the first set, and tried to get back that feeling and the sensations.
This is the only thing that I was just thinking of, no? Just tried to play back again as I was the first set. So tried to keep calm and be aggressive, but of course at the same time you cannot be very aggressive. Is very windy, and many times you need to adjust. Even like that, it was hard. So just to play point by point and try my best.

Q. Considering the place and the opponent, how do you rank the importance of this victory?

FERNANDO VERDASCO: Well, I mean, is very important. Obviously always beating a player like

Rafa is the same like if you beat, I mean, Murray or Federer or these guys. Is one of the biggest victories that you can have in tennis.

Of course is a huge victory, and it's always really nice to feel, you know, in a packed stadium or almost packed stadium in a very important tournament like this one and playing against one of the best players in history.

You know, at the end you just try to enjoy the moment also. Not even winning or losing. You always try to win, but enjoy the moment.

And I think that, you know, with the years you know more about that. When I was playing in these kind of conditions with 21 or 22 years old, it was different mentality than now.

So is what I'm trying to do, and today was a good day. I played good and I win, so what can I say? I'm very happy, and now I just need to try to rest and be ready for the next one.

Q. So when you enter a match playing a top player like Rafa, do you do anything different mentally to prepare yourself going into that kind of match?

FERNANDO VERDASCO: Well, just the adrenaline and, you know, like everything about a match like the one today, you don't even need to almost warm up. Just thinking about what kind of match are you going to play, your body is pumped, is ready for that.

Of course you try to make some stretching, try to move a little bit, but you need it much less than in maybe another match, a regular match.

So it's always like, you know, like special, special mentality. You know that you are playing against one of the best. You don't have, at the end, nothing to lose. He's the one that normally, when you play not only with Rafa, I say like when you play somebody like him, even with Roger or Novak or all these guys, normally they supposed to win against one player like me.

So I just try to give my best. Sometimes, you know, of course less times than I would like to I finish with victory, but every time I try, no? And today was one of these days, of course.

So I need to enjoy it so much, but at the end, the experience told me already when you have a victory like this one, you know, you need to be very careful. You need to stay still focused on the tournament.

It's not that you won the tournament already and you can go home. I still have more matches to come. The next one is in two days, so I need to keep focused on the tournament. You know, your friends are asking all the time, Are you going to celebrate? I say like, Not yet. If I go to celebrate today and tomorrow, then the next day I'm going to lose for sure.

It's tough, no, that part in tennis, but I'm happy anyways.

Q. One of the things that Rafa mentioned at his press conference was that he's not playing with as much freedom or he feels like nervous since he's come back. This is like the 15th time that you've played. Did you sense from your part that something was different from your past experiences with him?

FERNANDO VERDASCO: Well, we played each other many times, and everything happened. I mean, in 15 times, also the times that we played each other before being professional, when we were kids. I mean, 15, 17, 16. Everything happen in our matches. He beat me like 0 and 1 in finals of Monte-Carlo, and then another one was 7-6, 6-7, 7-6.

You know, and at the end, since last time that I beat him in Madrid, it was 13 times in a row for him. Some very easy and some of them for me having even match points.
The feelings, I mean, every match is different. Some matches you feel unbelievable. Some matches you don't feel that good. And the match of today, of course the conditions was not easy to play. I mean, the wind was tough. It was moving the ball around all the time. It was tough for him. It was tough for me.

But I guess that today I adapt myself better than him

in the day. He normally is one of the players, what I think, that is one of the best with these kind of wind. I saw him beating, for example, the finals in Indian Wells a few years ago Andy Murray like 6-2, 6-1, and it was unbelievable windy.

I know he's a tough player when it's windy like today, but maybe today he was not feeling good. I don't know. I'm not inside of him. So that's him, the one that needs to say about his feelings, not me.

What I saw is that of course with this wind he was missing more than normal, but also I was missing also a lot when, you know, the ball was moving and it was not easy to adjust and hit the ball where you wanted to.

Nadal leads series 13-2

2003 Hamburg qualifying Carpet   Nadal 6-2, 7-5

2005 Doha   Hard   R16   Nadal   6-2, 6-4

2005   Stuttgart Clay   R16   Nadal 6-3, 6-2

2006 Queens Club Grass R16   Nadal 2-6, 7-6, 7-6 (3)

2007 Indian Wells Masters Hard R32 Nadal 6-4, 6-4

2008 Roland Garros Clay R16 Nadal 6-1, 6-0, 6-2

2009 Australian Open Hard   SF Nadal 6-7, 6-4, 7-6, 6-7, 6-4

2009 Rome Masters Clay QF Nadal 6-3, 6-3

2009 Madrid Masters Clay QF Nadal 6-4, 7-5

2010   Monte Carlo Masters   Clay F   Nadal 6-0, 6-1

2010   US Open   Hard QF   Nadal   7-5, 6-3, 6-4

2011   Cincinnati Masters   Hard R16   Nadal 7-6, 6-7, 7-6 (9)

2012   Barcelona   Clay   SF   Nadal 6-0, 6-4

2012   Madrid Masters   R16   Verdasco   6-3, 3-6, 7-5

2015   Miami Masters   R32   Verdasco   6-4, 2-6, 6-3

"I think he has the best mind on the Tour by far."

Guillermo Canas: "I remember we played twice. Obviously he kicked my ass and I don't have good memories [smiles]. No, I played Rafa three times. I played semifinal in Acapulco once. I played quarterfinal or third round in Rome. And final of Barcelona. But always he beat me."

Question: Tough match up for you?

Guillermo Canas: "Yeah, it was kinda tough. But the way I play and everything, with most of the players I can play my game. With him, we play, not almost similar, but he has more shots than me. In other words, I need to try something different. And when you start to do something different in your game you have the less chance than the normal but I know if I play my game he's gonna beat me anywhere and that's why, for me, he was really tough to play against him."

Question: Was Rafa the hardest guy for you to play?

Guillermo Canas: "Yeah, one of them. I think he has the best mind on the Tour by far. So far. I think he's a great competitor in everything. I saw him many times with a lot of pains, foot pains. But when he's on the inside of the court he's an incredible competitor. I don't think anyone on the Tour is better than him. He's the best."

Question: Lasting memory of Rafa on or off court?

Guillermo Canas: "I don't have many memories. I just saw him like a normal person. When he started he was a very good friend with (Carlos) Moya who was a good friend of mine also. So for me he was the normal guy, like if you do the same things, PlayStation with (Juan) Monaco, all the time they played together. I think for me it was he was not normal inside of the court - and normal outside. I think this is very difficult to find a superstar so good like him inside of the court but normal person outside of the court."

Nadal leads series 3-0

2005   Acapulco   Clay   QF   Nadal   7-5, 6-3

2005   Rome Masters Clay R16   Nadal 6-3, 6-1

2007   Barcelona   Clay   F   Nadal 6-3, 6-4

"Everyone was saying he will be a good player."

Tommy Robredo: "The first memory of Rafa...he was a kid practicing in Barcelona. I was watching him practice and everyone was saying he will be a good player. He was about fourteen."

Question: Your most memorable match with Rafa?

Tommy Robredo: "I don't know. In Bercy I had the chance to beat him once and it was a really good match and then I lost it and it was great. I don't know. A lot of times I play against him. It's really tough to remember the most exciting one."

Nadal leads series 7-0

2005   Bastad   Clay SF   Nadal   6-3, 6-3

2005   Madrid Masters Hard   R16   Nadal   6-2, 6-4

2006   Barcelona   Clay   F   Nadal   6-4, 6-4, 6-0

2006   Tennis Masters Cup   China Hard RR   Nadal 7-6, 6-2

2009   Shanghai Masters   Hard R16   Nadal 6-1, 6-4

2009   Paris Masters   Hard R16   Nadal   6-3, 3-6, 7-5

2013   US Open   Hard   QF   Nadal   6-0, 6-2, 6-2

"He's a really true champion."

Radek Stepanek: "It's always a standout moment to play Nadal. We played seven, eight or nine times, maybe more. Always challenging, very much so. He's the biggest fighter on the Tour I have ever seen. Playing him, for me, is always good because he plays from the back of the court. I will try to create the play, not giving him much. I few matches I got really close, but never beat him. Yet. So I hope I will have the chance to play him still a few times."

Question: Your first memory of Rafael Nadal?

Radek Stepanek: "My first memory was we played in Davis Cup, deciding match in Czech Republic at two-all. For me, that moment was very disappointing loss because of, you know, playing as a team competition, which means a lot to me. So this was for me a tough defeat."

Question: Do you enjoy to play Rafa, or is it too difficult to be enjoyable?

Radek Stepanek: "Since I never beat him, it's difficult to play him. For everybody I think. I'm not the exception, we are all trying to beat him."

Question: Lasting memory of Rafa on or off court, that maybe captures his essence?

Radek Stepanek: "For me, a great fighter on the court. Biggest fighter ever. Great person also, off the court. He's very respectful to other guys, to all the players. He's a really true champion."

Nadal leads series 7-0

2004   Davis Cup Carpet First Round   Nadal   7-6, 7-6. 6-3

2005   Barcelona   Clay   SF   Nadal   7-5, 6-2

2005   Rome Masters   Clay   QF   Nadal   5-7, 6-1, 6-1

2005   Madrid Masters   Hard QF   Nadal 7-6, 6-4

2011   Queens Club   Grass   R1 6   Nadal   6-3, 5-7, 6-1

2012   Miami Masters   Hard   R32   Nadal   6-2, 6-2

2014   Indian Wells Masters   Hard R64   Nadal   2-6, 6-4, 7-5

"It's sad when he's not at the Grand Slam."

Benoit Paire: "Never easy to play against Rafa. But I like to play against him. Because he's one of the best players of the world. Not of the world, because he is. For me, when I played against him in Spain, it was a good moment because all of the crowd was supporting him. He's a very nice guy and it's sad for me when he's not at the Grand Slam, it's different without him."

Question: How did you feel about your performance vs. Nadal?

Benoit Paire: "As everybody knows it's very hard to play against Nadal. For me, I like to play against him. Because his forehand goes to my backhand - that's my best shot. But I never won one set. It was every time very difficult."

Question: Lasting memory or anecdote, on or off court of Rafa?

Benoit Paire: "Two years ago at Wimbledon I asked him for his autograph for my mom."

Nadal leads series 2-0

2013   Barcelona   Clay R16   Nadal 7-6, 6-2

2013   Madrid Masters Clay   R32   Nadal 6-3, 6-4

"He's a pure sportsman, a pure gladiator."

Dusan Vemic: "I played doubles against Rafa with Novak in 2009 in Montreal. Novak (Djokovic) was a little bit hurt. Rafa played with his coach (Francisco) Roig. I would have loved to get the win but it's okay [smiles]. It's always a special thing playing against some of the legends of tennis and that are still playing tennis and it's always a beautiful challenge. And actually I believe that everybody that is an underdog enjoys those moments and tries to bring the best out of them. To see if their best can challenge some of the top guys. For me, I always believed my serve was one of the best in the game. So the only thing I was thinking about when I played him is if my kick serve can bother his forehand. That's all I cared about. And there were like two or three kick serves that went over him and he mishit and I was really content and happy with my performance no matter what I did at the end. I think also we gotta enjoy those moments and embrace them."

Question: Did anything surprise you about Nadal being on the court competing against him?

Dusan Vemic: "No, no, no, he's just the way he is, he's an open book. Gives a hundred percent every single point, every single shot, he puts his heart into it. It's pretty much that simple."

Question: Lasting memory of Rafa on or off court?

Dusan Vemic: "Hmmm...that would take me a little while to think about. You could say he is someone all those little kids can look up to and really go down and then dig deep every single minute on the practice court. If he can do it - and he has achieved so much - then all of the little guys and girls can - twelve, fourteen, sixteen, eighteen - or even pros - can really look up to that kind of attitude. He's just a pure sportsman. A pure gladiator."

"He didn't want to let his buddy down."

Jean-Julien Rojer: "My first memory of Nadal...was the first time I played against him, I remember grandstand court in Miami tournament. Just a packed house. He comes out...just the whole thing. You see him do his rituals and stuff on TV, then the first time you actually play against him, and he's doing it in front of you. Just like to be very intimidating, jumping around everywhere. And brought a lot of intensity to the court. So that was my first memory of playing against him. This was three years ago 2011."

Question: What was your most memorable match with Rafa?

Jean-Julien Rojer: "That was the only time I played him. And that was quite memorable for me because I live in Miami. I grew up practicing there at that tournament and in Miami since I was twelve so I had a lot of friends and family there. Just how serious he took the match. He was playing with Marc Lopez, one of his best friends. And they really wanted to win. We ended up losing that match but it was a good match. Just such a great experience playing against him."

Question: Did anything surprise you about being on the court with him for the first time?

Jean-Julien Rojer: "Yeah, just how...I remember he made some mistakes. We just got the feeling that he wanted to win every single point, even in doubles. And he didn't want to let his buddy down. Him and Marc do great obviously, they won a few Masters

Series together. And they're both great players. Marc is a great player as well. But he just got so upset at little mistakes that he made in the doubles match, I think even more so than he would in a singles match. That to me was incredible, really."

Question: What was one of the mistakes Rafa made that you remember him getting annoyed at?

Jean-Julien Rojer: "I remember we were returning down the line a lot, trying to test his volleys and he normally has pretty good volleys for a guy that doesn't come in that much. But he has great hands and he made a mistake at the net and I remember he was shaking his head, went back, got the call from his partner, walked back to the net still shaking his head. So it was crazy."

Question: You're shot provoked that error?

Jean-Julien Rojer: "It was both actually. It was a sequence, it was my partner's shot he missed. It was a sequence where we returned three times consecutively up the line to him. And only one of the three volleys he missed. But that was the one that bothered him the most."

Question: Lasting memory of Rafa?

Jean-Julien Rojer: "Just a great presence. Fighter. Fighter mentality. Everything. I think of him, everything...the bandana, long hair, just coming at you at a thousand miles an hour. The relentless fighting every point. I think it's everywhere. You see him in the locker room, the way he walks, you know just how he is. The way he attacks life pretty much I guess."

"I've been killed in most of the matches."

Feliciano Lopez: "I beat Rafa two times. I beat Rafa in Queens 2010. I was playing very good, two sets, 76 64 against him. It was on grass which is my best surface. And this year I win. Everything was working perfectly. Since I went out on the court to play Rafa I was feeling great. I was feeling myself very smooth. And I think I played a great match. Probably top ten in my career. The other matches that we played I've been killed in most of them."

Nadal leads series 9-3

2003   Basel   Carpet   R32   Lopez   3-6, 6-3, 7-6 (4)

2006   Barcelona   Clay R32   Nadal 6-4, 6-2

2007   Stuttgart   Clay   SF   Nadal   6-1 7-5

2008   Barcelona Clay   R16   Nadal 6-4, 6-3

2008   Madrid Masters   Hard   QF   Nadal   6-4, 6-4

2009   Shanghai Masters   Hard   SF   Nadal   6-1, 3-0   RET

2010   Queens Club Grass   QD   Lopez   7-6, 6-4

2010   US Open   R16   Nadal   6-3, 6-4, 6-4

2011   Miami Masters   Hard R32   Nadal 6-3, 6-3

2011   Rome Masters   Clay R16   Nadal 6-4, 6-2

2012   Australian Open   Hard   R16   Nadal 6-4, 6-4, 6-2

2014   Shanghai Masters   Hard R 32 Lopez   6-3, 7-6 (6)

"Rafa heard that I was in Mallorca and contacted my coach."

Dusan Lajovic: "Well, it was a quick hour and a half. Three sets [smiles]. It was a great experience for me to play Nadal in Philippe Chatrier in Roland Garros I think in the fourth round, different then first and fourth so, for me it was a cherry on top of the cake for that tournament. Maybe it will even be better to play a different opponent in the fourth round to have maybe more chances but also you have to take from the positive side. I think that showed me how much more that I need to work and to improve to compete against these guys. So I think that was a great run two weeks in French Open. And if finished with even greater experience for me."

Question: Were you pleased with your performance vs. Rafa?

Dusan Lajovic: "I am. I am very pleased. And I kind

of had a very good draw there so I used it well and I think that when you play first time against one of the top, top Tour guys then it's always tough. I was really struggling to win points let alone games. So now I know how it is to play against this guy and then I hope that next time I will have little more chances."

Question: Did anything surprise you about being on court with Rafa for the first time?

Dusan Lajovic: "Well, yeah it surprised me how well that he anticipated the game and that even when you hit a 200 (kilometers) an hour serve, it doesn't really hurt him at all, which is something you really can look and see how he does it. It's amazing that he plays every point like the last one and this is one of his best, I think, best things that he has is that he's fighting. Doesn't matter if it's 61 50 or 60 50, he still wants to win every point. That's why he is there where he is."

Question: Talk about practicing with Rafa in Mallorca in the summer of 2014 and how the opportunity came to you?

Dusan Lajovic: "My second physio Jose was in Mallorca. He lives in Mallorca. So I went there mainly to recover. The first four or five days I didn't even hit balls. I was injured and then after that I started practicing. Mallorca is not a big place. I was in on academy and Rafa heard that I was there so he contacted my coach and we set up a practice and we hit two days."

Question: So you got to know Rafa as a person outside of the hectic tournament environment?

Dusan Lajovic: "Yes I did. We practiced on hard

court which is slightly different than clay. I had, let's say, a little bit more insight with practice - it's different than playing a match against him obviously. It was a great experience which helped me. I learned a lot to see how he practices. That he practices with even more intensity than you see on the court when he's playing in the match. He couldn't play backhand, he could only play sides because of the injury (right wrist). But still he was practicing hard every day and hoping that he will be able to play the US Open. Unfortunately, he didn't. That's the mindset of a champion. Even if he's injured, he's practicing what he could. So a lot to learn for us when we are playing with that."

Question: Did Rafa share with you a different side of his personality outside of the ferocious competitor? Was he a friendly host?

Dusan Lajovic: "Yes, he was pretty friendly. And I think when you're practicing with these guys, they are normal persons. The difference between on the court and off the court is that between rallies and stuff, when we're resting, we get the chance to talk with them, which we don't do in the match. So everything else they do is quite the same."

Nadal leads series 1-0

2014 Roland Garros Clay R16 Nadal 6-1, 6-2, 6-1

"His mind was already set to be one of the best."

Davide Sanguinetti: "When I play him he was like sixteen years younger than me. So I was descending in my career and he was going, going up. But I play with him I think three times and I don't think I even won a set with him. So he was already tough by then."

Question: Was he the hardest guy for you to play?

Davide Sanguinetti: "I cannot say the hardest guy because I played with all the best, so he's one of the hardest."

Question: Any standout memories from the three matches with Nadal?

David Sanguinetti: "Well, it's tough to finish the point against him because he was running like everywhere. He was playing like two meters behind the baseline and he was hitting the balls really, really hard. So and with the spin it was tough to control the ball."

Question: Do you have a special memory of Nadal off court?

Davide Sanguinetti: "Off the court he's just a nice guy. He's a normal person. He talks, he laughs, he jokes, so it's great to be with him."

Question: Did anything surprise you about playing him?

Davide Sanguinetti: "No. He didn't surprise me because I knew he was going to be one of the best players. Even when he was younger, I saw him playing for the first time. His mind was already set to be one of the best players in the world. And he became so."

Question: What is your first memory of Nadal?

Davide Sanguinetti: "I remember when he was really, really young. He already set his mind. His mind was already set to be a real professional player, to be one of the best. And I guess this was one of his best strengths."

Question: Do you remember where it was that you first saw him?

Davide Sanguinetti: "I think he was like fourteen years old, maybe fifteen. And he was playing club matches in Germany. And I saw him play. And he surprised me already."

Nadal leads series   2-0

2004   Madrid Masters   Hard   R64   Nadal 6-2, 6-1

2007   Chennai   Hard   QF   Nadal 6-3, 6-2

"I could do nothing for three months."

Steve Darcis

Question: Can you share memories of your famous match with Nadal at Wimbledon?

Steve Darcis: "I have very good memories and very bad. In ten minutes everything was done. I played maybe one of the best matches in my life in front of the big crowd. That's why you play tennis - is to play on that court against those kind of players. And yeah I was enjoying so much   during the match. After the match it was tough. I received a lot of messages, a lot of press, everything. And I knew I could not play the second round match. So you have to say everything is fine but inside of you it's not fine. So it was a little bit difficult. I had many very difficult months right after. So it's not only good memories."

Question: You said your surgeon said you might not even play again because of the shoulder injury you received from diving and falling on the court. In your mind did you know you could still play professionally again or did you have doubts?

Steve Darcis: "I doubt everyday. After the surgery I had so much pain. I sat two months on the sofa. I couldn't lie down. I was sleeping like I was sitting on the sofa trying to sleep but I had pain every second. I couldn't do anything. I just had the baby at that time...I couldn't hold her. I couldn't hold a glass of water. I could do nothing for three months. So yeah, I had doubts every day."

Question: Your style of play is unique. Do you feel you have an advantage over other players because your style is different? That most players don't see your kind of style often?

Steve Darcis: "Yeah, it's true. Yeah, I think for me it's good, they don't like to play me so much because it's strange. I make a lot of slice, I come to the net."

Question: You're sort of like Fabrice Santoro?

Steve Darcis: "No, because he's more talented than me [laughs]. No, I try to mix a lot because it's tough now, the courts are fast, everybody's getting stronger. Like you said, it's tough but I actually manage with what I can do."

Question: Was there a key point in the Nadal match that you realized you could actually beat him?

Steve Darcis: "It was tough for him because I saw in the middle of the third that he was complaining with the knee. So I knew that it was my chance but before that I think it was okay, still a good performance because that was the first time he lost first round in a Slam. I think it was pretty big."

Question: What were the tactics that were working against Nadal, do you remember?

Steve Darcis: "Yeah, of course. But you know if you stay on the backhand and you try to play with him you have no chance. So you have to come to the net. You have to take risks. You have to attack all the time. It's tough to keep that level during one match. If you lose one set, physically it's very difficult because he's giving you so many balls back, so much energy during every point, like we play three sets and we play three hours and a half. So it was very tough physically, mentally, because you have to come to the net all the time. You have to keep your game in mind. I could do it that day but it's tough."

Series tied 1-1

2010 Doha Hard   QF   Nadal 6-1, 2-0 RET

2013 Wimbledon   Grass   R128   Darcis   7-6 (4), 7-6 (8), 6-4

"I talked a bit of golf with him before the match."

Thanasi Kokkinakis: "I played him at the Aussie Open, second round. I was impressed by all the intensity and effort that he put into every ball that he hit. And I actually found his serve really awkward, it moved a lot. Had a lot of slice on his serve. Those were the big things. Tough to win a point against him."

Question: Before the match, how did you feel going out to the court to face the ATP World Tour number one player?

Thanasi Kokkinakis: "I wasn't nervous, I was more excited. I had already got the win in the first round. I had no pressure. So I went out there to try to swim freely. I knew obviously it was going to be a tough out but I did think I could trouble him a bit with my game style, the way I play. So I had a good chance in the second set to maybe break his serve or be close but I didn't take my break points. And, you know, it was suddenly one break at the end of that set. So it was pretty tight."

Question: Did anything surprise you about him?

Thanasi Kokkinakis: "Probably how well he handled my first serve. My first serve return, those were the main things. But apart from that I kind of expected most of it."

Question: Before the match how would you describe his preparations in the locker room?

Thanasi Kokkinakis: "Fine. I think I talked with him a bit about golf. I think there was golf on TV. So my coach and I talked a little bit of golf with him [smiles]. And that was probably about an hour before the match. But then obviously when we got closer he started getting prepared, like every other player."

Question: Lasting memory of Nadal on or off court?

Thanasi Kokkinakis: "He's been a nice guy to me. I enjoyed playing him, sharing the court with him. Hopefully next time it will be more fun and I'll come out on the other end."

Question: What will you try to do different next time?

Thanasi Kokkinakis: "Probably keep my first serve percentage up, he likes playing against second serves. And just keep giving it to him and being more aggressive and I'll be a lot more tougher physically next time around if I play him again."

Nadal leads series   1-0

2014 Australian Open   Hard   R64   Nadal 6-2, 6-4, 6-2

"Extremely focused and competitive but in a humble sort of way."

Matthew Ebden: "I played him on the grass courts right after he had won the French Open, so he'd come straight from Roland Garros. And to play him at Queens Club, first match on the grass while I'd had a few matches - I'd qualified and I'd won a round - and then I had to play him and it was his first match on grass. So it was a real good chance for me if there was ever gonna be the best chance to get him but I still lost 64 64 and it was one break each set. But he's Rafa, even after winning the French, being tired, coming on the grass, he still was able to beat me. So it wasn't too good for me. But yeah, he's a typical, you come out there, you see his ball fizzing around. And even though it's grass he still hits the ball unbelievable and super heavy."

Question: Did anything surprise you about being on court with him his first match on grass?

Matthew Ebden: "I'd hit with him a couple of times before. I remember just in the warmups, the first couple minutes, hitting up and down, his ball is very different to everyone else. It fizzes a lot higher and the shape and everything is a lot more through the air. But after a minute or two you adjust to it and it's fine. But just that initial sort of fizz through the air of his ball is different. You don't see that."

Question: Lasting memory of Rafa?

Matthew Ebden: "I guess it's his tenacity. Just the way he is humbly, extremely, completely...he's extremely focused and competitive but on himself more so, in a humble sort of way."

Nadal leads series   1-0

2011   Queens Club   Grass   R32   Nadal 6-4, 6-4

"He's not like 'killer' player, he wants to play rallies."

Lukas Lacko: "I played him a couple of times, maybe four or five times. I won one set only so that's the biggest memory, that I beat him 60 the one set. But otherwise it was very tough to play against him. Mostly I play him at Grand Slams, first or second or third round."

Question: Is Rafa the hardest guy to play for you?

Lukas Lacko: "Tough to say. Because when you play him you know it's not going to be like a fast match, quick match, you're not going to be outplayed like badly. Because he's not like 'killer' player. He wants to play rallies. You know there are going to be some long rallies. Compared to some other guys I played - I played with Roger twice - he's playing like...it's much harder to play against Roger, Roger plays aggressive. When he's on fire, normally it's no chance. With Rafa, when you play normally there are some chances because there are always rallies but still he's much better in these rallies that he plays. Against other players the rallies are much shorter. For me, it's like the biggest difference between like top players. You play Rafa, you know you are going to play. You play other top players which are on fire, it can be much shorter."

Question: You bageled Rafa, what happened there?

Lukas Lacko: "Actually, the kind of set...I served well. Three games I just served well. And three games like, every shot I touched was going in like, to the line. Everything was in my favor. It can happen. That can happen in two or three sets in one year. And it was good that it was against Rafa."

Question: Lasting memory or Rafa on or off court?

Lukas Lacko: "Nadal, off the court, he's very friendly. He always shakes hand, we talk like one or two questions. On court, I mean, he's very focused. Even if he's like 40-love down in the game, you have to fight for this game till the end."

Nadal leads series 4-0

2010   Australian Open   Hard   R64   Nadal 6-2, 6-2, 6-2

2011   Doha   Hard R16   Nadal   7-6, 0-6, 6-3

2012   Australian Open   Hard   R32   Nadal   6-2, 6-4, 6-2

2012   Halle   Grass R16   Nadal   7-5, 6-1

"He always gives you a chance to play good."

Teymuraz Gabashvili: "Well, I played him like four times. Probably the most memorable is here US Open 2010, night match. Because it was a great match, we played two tiebreaker sets, he only, I think, broke me once. I was in great form hitting the ball well. He was able to raise his game in the big moment."

Question: First memory of Rafa as a person?

Teymuraz Gabashvili: "I know him since I was young. He's only one year younger than me but we played the same tournaments since I was fourteen, thirteen. So I have long memory of him. When we were kids I was playing very well also I was number one or number two in the world as a kid. My first memory is when I met him first. Yes that's it [smiles]."

Question: Is Rafa the hardest for you to play?

Teymuraz Gabashvili: "Well it's tough to play because maybe the hardest guy as an opponent who doesn't give you the rhythm. Kind of players like maybe (Jerzy) Janowicz, (Robin) Soderling, who hit for power and he doesn't know what to do. He doesn't know what to expect from them. And if you have a crazy game like (Alexander) Dolgopolov...it's different because he doesn't play normal tennis. It's different with Nadal, he always gives you a chance to play good. But he's playing as a very strong player, he feels like an animal on the court. You have to always be concentrated and when you're playing on the stadium it can be like for five hours so it can be extremely difficult. So of course he's one of the toughest guys on the big tournament like Grand Slams because he has the fitness ability that is like amazing. But maybe it's not only because of fitness, because he wants it, he's used to working like this since like a kid, for every ball, fighting. So that's why he's now doing the same. So of course he's one of the most difficult players today."

Question: Do you remember the first match against him as a kid?

Teymuraz Gabashvili: "No. I never played him as a kid. First match against him was, where was it...either Miami or Roland Garros. I think it was Roland Garros. I don't remember '09 or '08, maybe second round. And I remember it was like 61 61 64 and we played more than three hours. You know it looked so easy but we played really long. Every game was deuce/advantage but I was never winning the games. So, you know, the game shows that in the most important moment he plays even better.   That's why it's tough to beat him. So yeah, it was a difficult match. He won. No, it was the year he lost against Soderling actually. So, yes that was my first match against him."

Nadal leads series 4-0

2009   Miami Masters   Hard   R64   Nadal 6-2, 6-2

2009   Roland Garros Clay R64   Nadal 6-1, 6-4, 6-2

2010   US Open   Hard   R128   Nadal   7-6, 7-6, 6-3

2014   Monte Carlo Masters   Clay   R32   Nadal   6-4, 6-1

"Even in the tough situations he finds a way to win."

Andre Sa: "The toughest competitor. The way he plays and fights for every point...it's a joke, really [smiles]. I played him in the Olympics in 2004 in Athens. That was the first time - I think he was seventeen - coming on the Tour. Tough kid. Competitive as hell. He tries to play as hard as he could every point, fighting for every point, which is normal for a seventeen year old at that time. Just the way he competes. He tried hard for every point. Big shots all over the place. In big moments, that's when he rises and plays his best tennis. That's what true champions do. And I played against him in Madrid, a few years after the Olympics. And even on doubles - after playing singles - he comes out for doubles playing so hard and so ready to play and to compete. That's what stood out for me in those two tries."

Question: His desire and hunger...where does it rank? Of all the people you have competed against, does anyone have more desire and hunger than Rafa?

Andre Sa: "I don't think so. I think he's the best of that. Even in the tough situations, he finds a way to win. You see other guys whining and moaning but he's always in his game and trying as hard as he can.

Trying to change things on the court, which, to me, makes it seem like he's really thinking about how to win the match. And, for me, definitely the best competitor out there."

Question: Anything surpise you about being on the court with him as opposed to being on the side or watching on TV?

Andre Sa: "No, no, it's just the way he is, even outside the court, he's just as competitive as can be playing every single game in the locker room, you want to play cards, whatever, he just wants to win. That's his motivation I guess."

Question: You compete against him in other things?

Andre Sa: "Yeah, everything, PlayStation, little mini, we play football together sometimes with a tennis ball on the court. The guy, as you can see, is going a hundred percent. Just the way he is on the court."

Question: Lasting memory of Rafa on or off court?

Andre Sa: "One time I remember after he won the French Open for the fourth or fifth time he came to Queens for the first year and everybody thought he's gonna come up and be so loose and relaxed...this was Monday afternoon. He won the French yesterday - the day before - and he was there doing the whole routine warming up like nothing happened. That shows that he's at another level. To me, sometimes when I won big matches, I mean, you're dead. Or you play Davis Cup, you're dead for the next couple of days. The guy was there, normal routine, playing doubles. He signed in for doubles to play Tuesday and then his singles on Wednesday. So I mean that just shows how competitive and professional he is."

Question: Best player of all time?

Andre Sa: "Tough to say. Tough to say. Roger I think is still a little bit better to watch, just the way he plays, how smart he is. But Rafa is definitely one of the greatest, maybe second greatest, best competitor for sure. I think he does that better than Federer. I know sometimes Federer is having a bad day, he loses. He doesn't really try to find a way to win the matches. He's just having a bad day. Rafa - he changes things around. Just try to compete better. So it's tough to pick between the two."

"I was waiting for him ten minutes to be ready."

Rainer Schuettler: "Well, I guess like most of the players who have played against him say, it's physically very tough. He's, for me, especially with the two-handed backhand, was not easy to get the high balls from his forehand side. So that was always very tough for me. And he's physically so strong and he's playing so well, he has no weaknesses, he goes to the net, he's worked on his backhand and also backhand on the run he's playing well. So for sure one of the toughest opponents you can get on the Tour."

Question: What is your first memory of Nadal?

Rainer Schuettler: "I played him when he came up when he was sixteen and I remember my first impression - he tries to hit everything as hard as he can already in the warmup. So I, of course, heard about him, he's one of the future stars. Then I played him and he really did everything in the warmup, he hit everything as hard as he could."

Question: What is your most memorable match with Nadal?

Rainer Schuettler: "That's a tough one. I beat him once at Basel in 2003 or 04, it's a long time ago. Of course I always try to remember the positive part. Otherwise, we played a few times, of course Wimbledon semifinal he beat me in three sets. But it was probably the most memorable."

Question: Is Rafa the hardest guy to play?

Rainer Schuettler: "For sure one of the hardest guys to play. As I said, he's lefty. It was always tough for me to play against him   because of the spin, the angle he could play with his forehand, so it was for sure one of the hardest guys for me to play."

Question: Lasting memory of Rafa?

Rainer Schuettler: "Just like everybody realizes, I played him once in Dubai and I think I was waiting for him like five minutes or ten minutes because all his routine had to be ready - his hair has to fixed and everything [smiles]. So his shoes have to be tied. So this was, for me, funny because I was waiting for him ten minutes to be ready [laughs]."

Nadal leads series 5-1

2004   Basel   Carpet   R32   Schuettler   6-3, 6-4

2005   Miami Masters   Hard   R64   Nadal 6-4, 7-6 (5)

2006   Dubai   Hard   SF   Nadal   6-4, 6-2

2007 Chennai   Hard   R32   Nadal 6-4, 6-2

2008   Wimbledon   Grass   SF   Nadal   6-1, 7-6, 6-4

2010   Indian Wells Masters   Hard   R64   Nadal 6-4, 6-4

"Magic shots in the big moments."

Andrey Golubev: "Our match was here in Arthur Ashe. It was for me a good experience. I played the number one, or number two at that moment I don't remember, but before the game I didn't know exactly why he's number one. After this game I understand for some reasons."

Question: What surprised you about Nadal in that match?

Andrey Golubev: "I was surprised that he was taking

every ball and getting it back. With most of the guys normally, you win the point. With him he gives back the ball when normally the point is over. So you don't expect, so he's getting balls back that surprise you. You can call it like magic shots in the big moments."

Question: So you entered this match with the belief you possibly had the chance to upset him?

Andrey Golubev: "Yes, of course. And I had my chance. I had seven set points. I was 5-2 - a double break in the other set. And in the moment he played like unbelievable. That's why I saw he was number one for that long and he won so many Grand Slams. So in those moments I just keep doing the same things and he just changed it and played like unbelievable."

Question: Is he the hardest guy for you to play?

Andrey Golubev: "Ahhh...I think...I mean, I played them all, like big four and for me the toughest was Federer."

Question: Why?

Andrey Golubev: "Because he can do everything. And with Rafa, I think, at least you play. You may lose 60 60 60 but you have this feeling that you play, that you were in the match, that it was some nice rally shots. With Federer, I mean, you can lose like 63 64 and you have feeling like you have no chance at all."

Question: Lasting memory of Rafa on or off court?

Andrey Golubev: "Off court, you can say he's a little bit shy guy. So he always says hello, how are you, speaking with the other players. And on court he's just like transforming into like an animal, you know [smiles]."

Question: How is Nadal before the match in the locker room?

Andrey Golubev: "Quite nervous. He warms up with the music. And he looks like nervous but in good perspective."

Question: Like a prizefighter?

Andrey Golubev: "Yeah, yeah. While Federer is like so relaxed, it's like he was just sitting there. Just take the bag and go on the court. Nadal is not doing like that. Of course, he's warming up but...and getting his mind and body ready for a big match."

Nadal leads series   1-0

2011   US Open   Hard R128   Nadal   6-3, 7-6, 7-5

"I'd say he runs too much."

Denis Istomin: "We played here at US Open in 2010 I think second round. Good match. I have a chance in the tiebreak second set, I was leading 5-1 and then I lost. But it was a good memory, for me, that match."

Question: Do you enjoy the process of playing Nadal or is it too physically grueling to play him to enjoy?

Denis Istomin: "I'd say he runs too much and I didn't really enjoy because I only won like five games. But it's really difficult to play against him. You have to be, first of all, physically a hundred percent and mentally you have to stay strong and fighting with him because he never gives even one point easy, you know. You have to be like so good and fight to win a point. Of course, a good spin he has. On forehand. Tough to make the winner against him. So he's not easy to play."

Question: Were there any tactics you were able to do that you felt were successful against him?

Denis Istomin: "The only way to beat him, you have to stay close to the baseline and just try to play aggressive and trying to move him and going to the net. So that's the only way. If you give him a chance, then no chance for you."

Question: Lasting memory or Rafa on or off court?

Denis Istomin: "I mean, he's a nice guy. Very talented and everybody can see how he's working on the court and out of the court. He always impress himself. And very friendly. Good charisma. He's a great player and a great person."

Nadal leads series 4-0

2010   Queens Club   Grass R16   Nadal   7-6, 4-6, 6-4

2010   US Open   Hard R64   Nadal   6-2, 7-6, 7-5

2012   Roland Garros   Clay R64   Nadal   6-2, 6-2, 6-0

2014   Miami Masters   Hard   R32   Nadal 6-1, 6-0

"He said I have to become much more physical, with more intensity."

Juan Sebastien Gomez practiced with Nadal at 2010 US Open...

On Wednesday, less than 24 hours after defeating Feliciano Lopez in straight sets on Tuesday night on Ashe Stadium, Rafael Nadal enjoys a hit with Juan Sebastien Gomez, a junior player from Colombia. I spoke with Gomez moments after he traded shots with the world number one on court P1 from 2-3 in the afternoon...

Question: How did you get the opportunity to hit with the great Rafael Nadal?

Juan Sebastien Gomez: "My trainer contacted Carlos Costa (Nadal's agent) to hit with him. And I start to play with Rafa. That's why."

Question: First time you play with Rafa?

Juan Sebastien Gomez: "This is the third time that I have hit with him during the US Open. Third time. It's amazing."

Question: What have you learned?

Juan Sebastien Gomez: "I learned the acceleration of the ball. The weak shot, when he have it, the ball disappears."

Question: What do you mean?

Juan Sebastien Gomez: "When I hit the weak shot, he accelerate so fast and the ball disappears – it's a winner. My ball so slow, and it's a winner for him. I learn it and I really like that. It's amazing."

Question: Did you talk with Rafa at all?

Juan Sebastien Gomez: "Yes, I talk with him. He tells me about the physical, that he trains a lot in the court, with the intensity of him – he is very physical. He said I have to move much better, faster. I have to become much more physical, with more intensity."

Question: What else has stood out about sharing a court with Rafa Nadal?

Juan Sebastien Gomez: "The experience is amazing to hit with him. It's unbelievable and I want to hit another time with him."

Question: Let me ask you this – who will win the US Open?

Juan Sebastien Gomez: "I think will win…Rafael Nadal will win the tournament. First, because I am training with him [laughs]. And because he's very gifted and he's hitting the ball incredible. I think Rafael Nadal will win."

Question: You think Nadal will beat Federer?

Juan Sebastien Gomez: "Yes. I think Nadal will beat another time, Federer."

Question: And last, what is the most memorable aspect about hitting three times with Rafa Nadal?

Juan Sebastien Gomez: "That it's a good experience. And he's friendly. I like the humor of him. I like."

(Nadal won the 2010 US Open by defeating Novak Djokovic 64 57 64 62.)

"He had such intensity at fifteen."

Attila Savolt: "I had a practice with Nadal when he was fifteen. He was unbelievable. He was hitting the ball so hard that day. Just at a practice. That was maybe 2002 or 2003 at a Challenger in France, like $150,000 Challenger. And we just hit the balls for an hour. And he was hitting unbelievable. And he had such an intensity and everything already at the age of fifteen. He was like a full player. Normally at the age of fifteen, you're playing the junior tournaments, you're acting kind of like a junior and everything. He was already so professional. He already knew what he was doing so much. And he was so dedicated."

"He's an animal."

Stefan Koubek: "Nadal's an animal. He looks like one and plays like one [smiles]. But he's a really nice guy I have to say. I only practice with him but there's a lot of power behind his shots."

"His serve hit Lopez in the back of the head and bounced out of the stadium."

Eric Butorac: "Never lost to Nadal. I played him once in Indian Wells [smiles]. I remember his forehand. I never met somebody that hit a forehand that actually moved that much, like, vertically. Like, I thought I was about to hit a ball and it landed down at my shoes. It wasn't so much the speed through the air, it was the amount that it dips."

Question: Lasting memory of being on the court with Nadal?

Eric Butorac: "He hit (his partner) Feliciano Lopez in the back of the head with a serve 130 miles an hour, off his head - and it went out of the stadium [smiles]."

"It's a pain in the ass to play the guy."

Dustin Brown: "I played really well (beating Nadal at Halle in 2014). I served well. And I returned pretty aggressive and I didn't make a lot of mistakes. And I really didn't let him play his game."

Question: Stepping on the court with Rafa as the decided underdog, when did you first begin to believe you could win the match?

Dustin Brown: "From the beginning I was just trying to serve well and stay in there. And after a while - there was one close service game at, I think, 3-all or 3-2, which I held. And then I realized I had chances on his serve, even more and more. And, yeah, I just tried to stick to the gameplan. And once I started playing better and returning well, then, of course, the confidence came, especially after winning the first set."

Question: How did your life and career change after that win?

Dustin Brown: "Not at all [smiles]. Why would it change? It's still only one tennis match."

Question: The whole tennis world saw that match.

Dustin Brown: "Yeah, of course, nothing changed compared to money or ranking. It's one match. It makes no difference if it was Nadal or I was playing a wildcard. For me, personally, the confidence and playing well of course, but besides that nothing really changed."

Question: Describe the feeling of being on the court with Nadal?

Dustin Brown: "Well, the beginning I was a little awkward because most of the time you see him playing on TV. The week before he won the French Open. And then when I was on the court, it's a real pain in the ass to play the guy and just try to do my best and yeah, it worked out really well."

Question: Did you become a different player after that match? How did you do after that match?

Dustin Brown: "Well, of course, going on the court I had more confidence. But like I said, it's only one tennis match. I lost a pretty close one the match after to (Philipp) Kohlschreiber. So it was nothing really changed."

Question: Was that the best tennis you ever played? Versus Rafa?

Dustin Brown: "Yeah, that was a pretty perfect day [smiles]."

Brown leads series 1-0

2014   Halle   Grass   R16   Brown   6-4, 6-1

"Work, work, work, never give up."

Alejandro Gonzalez: "I practiced with Rafa when I was a junior. I remember, for sure, it was a fun experience for me, that moment with a professional, with Nadal. The guy was very nice in that moment and very cool."

Question: At the French Open?

Alejandro Gonzalez: "Yes, eight years ago."

Question: Did anything surprise you about being on the court with him?

Alejandro Gonzalez: "No. I used to see him play a lot, practicing. And, of course, in that moment, his ball was really heavy. When you are a junior, that surprises you."

Question: At that practice, Rafa generally was probably focused on business and getting ready for a big match, did he manage to be helpful to you in any way?

Alejandro Gonzalez: "He was getting ready for his match against Djokovic in the quarterfinal (2006). He was also helpful for me. Like I said, when you practice with a pro like Nadal and you are a junior, it's something cool. I remember he told me, 'Work, work, never give up. To keep working when you have a dream.'"

Question: Have you seen Rafa since? Any interactions?

Alejandro Gonzalez: "Of course, I'm a pro also. During the tournaments I see him a lot."

Question: Keep in touch? Talk?

Alejandro Gonzalez: "No, no [smiles]. Not really."

Question: It's more business?

Alejandro Gonzalez: "Yeah. Everyone in the sport looks his own way."

Question: What did you learn about Rafa on the court?

Alejandro Gonzalez: "Nadal, he's a good player. I think the things everybody admires about him is his attitude. And it's something very positive that he has."

Question: Lasting memory of Rafa?

Alejandro Gonzalez: "That he's a normal human. And another player. But mentally he's very strong and positive."

"He was born to play tennis I think."

Ruben Ramirez Hidalgo: "When you see one guy like Nadal, when he's young you can see that he's gonna play so good. Because they have some unbelievable things for young people that is so good."

Question: What qualities did you see?

Ruben Ramirez Hidalgo: "The mentality. Like always fighting and always saying 'Come on' and fighting every ball. You can see inside him everything."

Question: Is Rafa the most intense player you've ever seen or played against?

Ruben Ramirez Hidalgo: "For me, yes. Yes. And not because he's a Spanish guy. He's unbelievable."

Question: First memory of Rafa?

Ruben Ramirez Hidalgo: "Yes, I heard about him. And I saw him one time at a Futures tournament. He was so down. I watch the game. He was playing with a guy three or four years older than him. And he was fighting in all the games all the points. And you can see this guy is gonna be so good."

Question: You just knew then he would be a great champion?

Ruben Ramirez Hidalgo: "Yes, yes [smiles]."

Question: When you played him in the court in 2002 and 2003 did anything surprise you about him?

Ruben Ramirez Hidalgo: "I remember I lost to him in the Challenger and he won the tournament - his first Challenger tournament. I think he was sixteen or seventeen."

Question: Are his shots special? Or is it more his extraordinary desire and intensity?

Ruben Ramirez Hidalgo: "Everything I think. He's born to play tennis I think."

Question: Do you think he's the greatest player of all time?

Ruben Ramirez Hidalgo: "Ah yes, I think so."

Question: Because Federer has not been able to solve his game.

Ruben Ramirez Hidalgo: "Yes. Federer is also an unbelievable guy."

Question: You almost beat Federer in Monte Carlo in 2008.

Ruben Ramirez Hidalgo: "Yes. I lost. I was up 5-1 in the third set and then I lost [smiles] in a tiebreaker. This is tennis. Federer is also a great player, a solid player."

Question: Which one is harder for you to play?

Ruben Ramirez Hidalgo: "Both [laughs]. You can't say one or the other. Because these two guys are so good."

Nadal leads series 2-0

2003   Barletta Italy   Clay R32   Nadal   7-6, 6-3
2003   Aix En Provence France   Clay   SF   7-5, 6-2

"Great guy off the court."

Donald Young: "It's tough to play Nadal. He doesn't give away any points. He competes hard and he hits the ball heavy. Just gets to everything. Just a really tough out."

Question: Toughest to play?

Donald Young: "Hmmm...for me Andy Murray is tough to play. He just does everything so well. And such a strong base. He's a tough player."

Question: You played Nadal once. What is he like before the match in the locker room?

Donald Young: "He's a nice guy. Great guy off the court. Before the match he's pretty serious. On the court he's really intense. But off the court and before the match he's a great guy."

Question: Did anything surprise you about playing Nadal?

Donald Young: "No. It was everything I expected and saw on TV. Besides actually feeling the ball yourself is something you can't see on the TV, you could only feel."

Question: Who has the best forehand you faced?

Donald Young: "There's a ton. I practiced with (Fernando) Gonzalez. Rafa. I played Fed(erer). Fed's was pretty good. I couldn't read it at all. I played Jack Sock, he has a good one. A lot of good ones. Most everybody has a good one."

Question: Lasting memory or anecdote of playing Nadal, being on the ATP World Tour with him?

Donald Young: "Just professional. Really professional. Hard-working professional."

Nadal leads series 2-0

2008 Indian Wells Masters Hard R32 Nadal 6-1, 6-3

2015 Indian Wells Masters Hard R32 Nadal 6-4, 6-2

"He moves like a guy that's smaller."

Michael Russell: "I played him once. I practiced with him a few times. Tough competitor. He's not gonna give you an inch. He runs for every ball. Enormous racquet head speed, more than anybody in the history of the game. And he really uses that to his advantage. He's able to create spins and angles that you just don't see."

Question: Before the match, what is he like? I was told by one player he does windsprints in the locker room.

Michael Russell: "He'll warm up. The funny thing is he actually takes forever to warm up. If you're supposed to play at two o'clock, you might as well wait to 2:15 because he takes forever to warm up. He doesn't tape his ankles or his fingers until they actually call the match. So you really gotta be prepared to wait a little bit. And, you know, he does all his little jumps at the net. He's got a lot of energy. But obviously that's why he's one of the greatest players of all time."

Question: Did anything surprise you about being on the court with him?

Michael Russell: "Well, I see him at every tournament so I know a lot more about him than other people. A lot of people don't realize he's actually pretty big, he's almost 6-foot-2. But he moves like a guy that's smaller. A lot of people don't realize he's still tall and he has a lot of leverage. And that's one of the things that surprises people the most."

Question: Describe what it's like to practice with him?

Michael Russell: "Just incredible intensity. We practiced a few times in Australia, once even before he had a match. And we hit a good forty-five minutes. Really good pace and energy. And he went out and played four sets, three and a half hours. So he's very fit, as we all know. And he takes that through his practice sessions into his matches. I'm the same way. The guys at the top of the sport - they do the same. You have to really go into every practice and treat it like a match. He's got such good focus."

Question: How is he to interact with? Do you have a good rapport with Rafa? Or is he all business?

Michael Russell: "No. He's very friendly. Especially him with the other Spanish guys. They have great camaraderie, they're laughing, they play games together, whether it's video games or card games. They really have a good clique. All of them. It's a close group of guys. So he's very friendly, down to earth."

Question: Lasting memory or anecdote of Nadal?

Michael Russell: "The first time I saw Nadal I was in Mallorca, where he's from, playing the ATP event. They had an ATP event in Mallorca in 2002. He was a kid. He was a wildcard. And a friend of mine, Ramon Delgado, played him first round. I remember he was sixteen (actually fifteen and ten months). So I was like, 'He's only sixteen. You have a pretty good draw.' And Ramon was like, 'I heard he's pretty good this player.' And we were watching him play. And he actually beat Ramon. And it was Rafael Nadal, lefty. And he wasn't nearly as tall. He had that really whippy forehand. And the rest is history. He ended up losing a pretty good match to Gaston Gaudio. And Gaston went on to win the tournament. It was just funny to see it. The kid was just sixteen years old and went on to have an incredible career. And to be that good at sixteen, to win an ATP level match."

Question: We may never see that again.

Michael Russell: "Very rare. I'd be very surprised."

Nadal leads series   1-0

2011   Wimbledon   Grass R128   Nadal   6-4, 6-2, 6-2

"The sense of belief, physicality."

Justin Gimelstob: "It's his energy, the spin, the sense of belief, his physicality, the way he tracks down balls. At the time we played, he stood much farther back behind the baseline. His serve wasn't very good. He didn't like being attacked. Like most of the great players I played in my career, I found a way to lose, he found a way to win. Since then he's gotten so much better."

Nadal leads series   1-0

2005   Beijing   Hard R16   Nadal   5-7, 6-4, 6-4

"He has good instincts for doubles too."

Daniel Nestor: "He's like a left-handed Jack Sock with the forehand (interview was done in Newport just days after Sock and Vasek Pospisil won the 2015 Wimbledon doubles title). Yeah, I mean the ball comes off Rafa's racquet huge. Both sides. He has good instincts for doubles too, which you wouldn't think because he doesn't play a lot. He's an amazing player. There's so much authority, it's like, the ball - you have that feeling it's knocking you off balance."

Question: Lasting memory or anecdote of Rafa on or off court?

Daniel Nestor: "Just a classy guy. Off the court he's a down to earth guy. A lot of the top guys have their entourages doing everything for them, but you get the feeling he's worked hard his whole life to get to the top and he hasn't forgotten where he's come from. That kind of feeling, he does things for himself, he doesn't need people doing things for him. Just a genuine guy. He always has time for people. And friendly. You wouldn't expect someone ranked number one in the world and dominated for so long to behave that way but he does. Which is nice."

Nadal leads doubles series 4-2

2010   Indian Wells F Nadal/M.Lopez vs. Nestor/Zimonjic   W 7-6, 6-3

2009   Doha   F   Nadal/M. Lopez vs. Nestor/Zimonjic   W   4-6, 6-4, 10-8

2008   Queens   R16   Nadal/Robredo   vs. Nestor/Zimonjic   W 5-7, 6-3, 10-3

2007   Barcelona QF Nadal/B. Salva-Vidal vs. Nestor/Zimonjic W 7-6, 6-3

2006   Madrid   R16 Nadal/F. Lopez vs. Nestor/Knowles   L 6-4, 5-7, 9-11

2005   Miami QF   Nadal/F. Lopez. vs. Nestor/Knowles   L   6-7, 6-7

"He's definitely beatable...but it's a tall task."

John Isner: "It's always a big experience because when you play him more times than not you're playing on the biggest stage of that particular tournament, so you always have a big crowd. It's certainly a tough challenge. He's one of the greatest players of all time."

Question: Your most memorable match with Rafa?

John Isner: "Probably when I played him at the French Open and I lost in five sets."

Question: Surprised you did so well against him on clay in that match?

John Isner: "No, no, I knew I could give him some, a little bit of trouble. I think I can give a lot of people trouble with how I play. So that was the case that day but he toughed me out."

Question: What's it going to take to beat Rafa?

John Isner: "You have to play aggressive. He's definitely beatable. I mean, all the guys are beatable. But it's a tall task though."

Nadal leads series 5-0

2010   Indian Wells Masters   Hard R16   Nadal   7-5, 3-6, 6-3

2010   Madrid Masters   Clay   R16   Nadal   7-5, 6-4

2011   Roland Garros   Clay   R128   Nadal   6-4, 6-7, 6-7, 6-2, 6-4

2013   Cincinnati Masters   Hard   F   Nadal   7-6, 7-6

2015   Monte Carlo Masters   Clay R16   Nadal   7-6, 4-6, 6-3

"He hits full power, every ball."

Dudi Sela: "I played him in juniors and once in ATP. We practiced together many times."

Question: What are your memories from the junior match?

Dudi Sela: "No memory. I don't remember [smiles]."

Question: Describe the feeling of hitting with Rafa.

Dudi Sela: "He hits every ball the same, like full power every ball. Everybody is going to tell you the same. He doesn't care so much in practice where the ball is going, it's more about his racquet speed, that it's moving. The hand is moving very fast. That's the way he's playing."

Question: The most difficult guy to play against?

Dudi Sela: "To play against Rafa - he's fit. He's fighting for every point. Almost no weaknesses. The backhand a little bit, he cannot hit a winner like Murray or Djokovic but it's different. The ball is bouncing very high on the hard court, especially these days with the hard courts very bouncy. So it's tough."

Nadal leads series   1-0

2015 Australian Open Hard   R32   Nadal 6-1, 6-0, 7-5

Chapter 3: Rafael Nadal Press Conference Interviews

(Photo by Scoop Malinowski.)

Miami Masters

March 28, 2004

Rafael Nadal speaks after his 63 63 defeat vs. Roger Federer

Q. How does it feel to beat the No. 1 seed?

RAFAEL NADAL: Yes, I'm very happy because I played one of the best matches in my life. Obviously, he didn't play his best tennis and that's the reason why I could win. I mean, if he had played his best tennis, I would have had no chance. But that's what happens in tennis. If a player like me plays at a very, very good level and a top player like Roger doesn't play his best tennis, I can win. But, sure, I'm really, really happy.

Q. (Inaudible)?

RAFAEL NADAL: Yeah, I played almost perfect tennis today because I was playing inside the court, dominating the exchanges and pressing him so he couldn't play his game. But one thing I forgot, I served extremely well today, probably I never served like this in my life. That was really the key.

Q. Everybody seems to be afraid to play Federer. You did not look like you were afraid.

RAFAEL NADAL: Yes, I mean, I was afraid that he could win 6-1, 6-1 or 6-1, 6-2 but I was really looking forward to playing this match because I was playing against the No. 1 player in the world. I went on court with a positive attitude, not with the attitude of, "Oh, let's try and win one game."

Q. How would you describe your playing style?

RAFAEL NADAL: When I play well, I'm a very aggressive player with a good forehand and I fight very hard on the court.

Q. Technically and tactically, what was the key of the match? How did you approach this match?

RAFAEL NADAL: Well, I knew that the most important point was that I couldn't let him play his own game, because if he can play his own game, he wins 6-1, 6-1, 6-1, 6-2 like it's happening this year and it's never happened in tennis before. So from the first point I knew that I had to dictate the exchange for him not to be able to play his game.

Q. How do you organize your day for practicing, for tactics of the matches if you are just on your own?

RAFAEL NADAL: No, I'm here with somebody, I'm here with Jofre Porta, who usually is with Carlos Moya, but Carlos Moya, he's here with Joan Bosch. I'm here with somebody that helps me. At the same time, before every match, I call my uncle and so we speak about the match.

Q. As you said, you served very well today. Did you change anything on your serve since last year?

RAFAEL NADAL: Yeah, it's mostly that every match I

try to hit my serve harder, and, you know, every match I play, because I think that's how you can improve yourself; you have to be more aggressive and go for it. That's the key. Obviously, I know I've changed my movement a little bit, but that's the key, going for it more. Like, for instance, last week, I served at 6-5 against Calleri in the third set, and I didn't serve hard, I served like slowly, and I lost it. So that's the key really.

Q. The way you played tonight, it suggests that you're not the kind of player who's going to be afraid of playing on any surface, whether it's hard court, clay, even grass. Is that your goal, to be playing on all the surfaces well?

RAFAEL NADAL: No, I've always said that I'm the kind of player that can play well on all surfaces. I played well on grass last year. I played well on hard court outdoors. I play well on clay, obviously, because I'm used to it; I grew up on clay. And maybe I didn't play well last year indoors, but it was mostly because it was the end of the year and, you know, I was little bit tired. It was my first year, and I was a little bit tired at the end of the year. If you're not in very good shape physically and mentally, you cannot compete at this level.

Q. Last year when you lost to El Aynaoui at the US Open, you said you didn't feel you belonged to that top level of tennis and that was the reason why you had lost. What's the difference now?

RAFAEL NADAL: Definitely, this year I have much more confidence and I know that I can play at that level, that I belong to the higher level of players.

Obviously, last year I was winning my matches because I was fighting very hard. This is the same this year, but I'm also winning because I raised my level and I believe I belong to the top.

Q. Do you think you could play that kind of level in a match in a Grand Slam tournament, the best-of-five sets?

RAFAEL NADAL: Well, I've only played like Wimbledon and I got to the third round, and then US Open I got to the second round and then in Australia I lost to Hewitt in three sets. So I only need to play Paris, which I haven't played before, and that's different there because it's clay courts. But I think that physically I'm not such a bad player.

Q. This is a result that's going to reverberate around the world. Do you think your mobile phone will be pretty busy with calls tonight, congratulations?

RAFAEL NADAL: No, not right now because it's 4 a.m. in Spain so everybody's sleeping. Tomorrow, the papers won't have this news. But, yeah, maybe Internet and on the teletext I will start getting some calls.

Q. You lost last year to Gonzalez, so what do you think about that match and tomorrow's match?

RAFAEL NADAL: Yeah, sure, I lost against him and it was in Stuttgart. I thought I played a good match, one of the best matches up to that point in my career. It was the first time that I played against somebody who hit the ball so hard. He was doing everything. I was just running around. I played well to win the second set, and then I lost in three sets. But I think tomorrow is going to be different because now I'm used to these kind of players.

Q. Your win today and Monaco's win over Guga yesterday were the same matches - you showed you're young players, hitting the ball very hard and dominating the other players. Is that the tennis of the future, and if your style of play doesn't work, do you have anything else to fall back on?

RAFAEL NADAL: Well, I don't think that Monaco or I discovered the world, because that's actually the way tennis players are playing right now, like Ferrero, Moya, Federer, Safin, you know, hitting the ball very hard. I'm particularly happy for Monaco because he's played well this year, especially in Buenos Aires and Brazil and here. I've known him quite well because he was training in Spain, so I've known him since the time he was playing futures in Spain.

Q. How important was it for you to play Davis Cup this year? How did it help you believe you are part of the top players?

RAFAEL NADAL: Yeah, it's true. Davis Cup was one of the best, if not the best experience so far. I was there, I lost my first two points, and then I won the last and it was just unbelievable. Obviously, now we have this match coming up in Mallorca. I would like to play again. But in Spain we have a lot of good players - Ferrero, Moya, who are ahead of me. I'm hoping to play maybe in the doubles, but the team is going to be announced on Tuesday.

Madrid Masters

October 19, 2004

Q. We've seen you play. You're improving every time. Is it a question of your personality? What is your football team? Your uncle supports Barca. Why do you Support Real Madrid?

RAFAEL NADAL: Well, maybe I'm improving because I'm fit now. Decided not to go to China, to train for the Davis Cup. I trained for a week very intensely in Mallorca. Then I won the semifinals in Mallorca. That's why I'm improving. I'm full of energy. Maybe I'll win, maybe I'll lose, but I'll give my best. Here I'm not as fit as I could be. That can be seen on the court. But the important thing is I finally won. My uncle supported the Barcelona football team, that's true, but I support Real Madrid. Although I have nothing against Barca because they treat me well, too.

Q. You told us yesterday this was going to be a tough match. It seemed quite easy, though. What happened?

RAFAEL NADAL: I don't know what to say. I guess, Sanguinetti has not had his best day. Although I was not playing that good. I started gradually to feel better during the training and today, this morning. I've tried to give my best. I played a serious match without many errors. Here with the altitude, the courts are quite fast. I think Sanguinetti has noticed that and has had problems. A player has to be used to fast courts.

Q. You have doubles now. Looking further ahead, what do you think about your match in the second round?

RAFAEL NADAL: I'm not thinking about that, I'm thinking about the match I have in a few minutes. It will be against Spadea. It will be a difficult match. I certainly will have to do better than today. But this match has given me confidence. I think I need it to win, because the last two matches I played, I lost. The week before, I lost by a lot, 6-3, 6-Love. That was something terrible because I couldn't win. There was no way of recovering in that match. So this has been a very important victory for me.

Q. If someone was to say that you had the physique of a Boris Becker and the spirit and determination of a Jimmy Connors, would you understand what they meant and would you take it as a compliment?

RAFAEL NADAL: I hope I have, of course, because those two players are great. If I was a mixture of both, I would be really high. If someone told me that, that could be a personal opinion. I'm thankful for the commentary. I hope it was this way, but I don't think so.

Q. What do you think this decline is due to? The post-Davis Cup?

RAFAEL NADAL: After the Davis Cup in Palermo, I went down. It was complicated. I think every player feels the same. To play the Davis Cup is an important stimulation, accumulated pressure because the doubles was very long, five sets. We were risking not to qualify. It's not easy to continue playing next week. Despite that, when I got there, I won a match, a proper match, I mean, more or less good play. Then I lost. It's not an excuse because my opponent was playing quite well, but the truth is I was not feeling well that day. I couldn't see the ball I turned to my teammates and said, "I cannot see." Well, it's not an excuse. He was superior. He defeated me. But I only prepared five days before. Not only. I mean, I prepared for five days. I wanted to give my best, but I couldn't. Sometimes those things happen. Maybe I was not confident enough. Palermo, change of surface. It was not like this. It was like in the Czech Republic. One could easily slide. I was not motivated nor confident enough to win the match that day.

Q. Yesterday you said you were really looking forward to play against Agassi. Now you have Spadea and then maybe Agassi. What do you think?

RAFAEL NADAL: Yeah, it would be great not only to play against him, but also the fact that the match would give me 75 points. My goal is to make it into the Top 20. I'm 40 or 45, around there. At least I will end better than last season. I would end with a few matches to my name that have been good. I would look forward especially to the Davis Cup, which is the most important thing we have ahead of us. However, I'd like to defeat Spadea, of course, and facing Agassi. Last of the options I have.

Australian Open

January 18, 2007

Q. Could you tell us where you got hit with those two balls, how badly it hurt. When Kohlschreiber hit you at the net with those two balls, where did it hit and badly did it hurt?

RAFAEL NADAL: The first one there in the finger. The other one I touch with the racquet. The first one I understand hundred percent fine. You are in the net, you want to win the point. But the second one is a little bit struggling because he has all court for him, no?

But it's fine.

Q. Where did the second one hit you?

RAFAEL NADAL: No, no. In the racquet.

Q. On the racquet?

RAFAEL NADAL: Yes. For very good luck on the racquet. For nothing put me in one eye, something, in the face.

Q. It was a good fight. Did you like it?

RAFAEL NADAL: Yeah, I am happy with this match, no? Was very important for me. Is very good test because I finish the match very good physically. The first set I play very good tennis, too. Kohlschreiber play a good match. Was playing great tennis. I just play bad maybe the final of third set, no? I serve bad. I play without confidence with my serve and with my forehand and backhand. I miss a lot. But it's fine, no? After I come back very well with very good attitude. I am very happy for that, no? I feel faster on court than the other days, no? Today I feel the faster day when I start this season, no? I am happy. Maybe I improve my tennis here. I feel better here than Shanghai right now. I have good confidence next round.

Q. Were you surprised by the way he played?

RAFAEL NADAL: No, I know every match is tough. You could see, Roddick was losing two sets to love against Tsonga. Safin two sets to one. When you are at the hotel and you saw the TV, when you go on court, you think, I going to have a difficult match, too.

Q. Does it give you confidence that you don't play your best and you still win?

RAFAEL NADAL: Well, that's very important, no? Is very important win when you're not playing the best because that's a good point. That give me very good confidence.

But I am happy with my game today. I feel better. Maybe is the first match in the year when I feel better,

I feel good in some moments, no? So that's very important. I am trying every day to get my hundred percent. But I am fine. I improving every day, so that's very important for me.

Q. Fans were very loud. Did the Spanish fans help you or did the German fans bother you at all?

RAFAEL NADAL: Everything is fine, no? The atmosphere was fine. Always here I play good matches here against Hewitt against one Australian. The people here is very nice, respectful with the game. Was nice. The German, the Spanish, so everything fine.

Australian Open 2007

After playing and defeating Stanislas Wawrinka for the first time

Q. Was it a harder match than the scores indicated?

RAFAEL NADAL: Yes, always. Every match is tough. Every match is different. Every match have difficult moments. But today maybe I won 6-2, 6-2, 6-2. But always the points are tough. But in every set I have 4-1 with two breaks, so that's important, no?

Q. Are you happy with your form going into the second week? Is this where you would like to be?

RAFAEL NADAL: Yeah, for sure I'm happy today. I play my best match, hundred percent. I play good today - very, very good. I'm happy for that.

Q. It was the first time you played Wawrinka. What do you think about him?

RAFAEL NADAL: Well, he has a very good shots. He serve well. Very good backhand. On the forehand sometimes irregular. So what? He's young, too. He can improve. He's No. 31 in the world right now, so that's very good number, and improving.

Q. If you play Murray next, how different will he be to Wawrinka, the challenge?

RAFAEL NADAL: A hundred percent different. He's a different player, different style, everything different. You can't compare the matches, no? We will see. If is Murray, is going to be very difficult match. If it's Chela, too. We will see Murray's improving his game. He's very young. Just one less than me, yeah. Well, he start good the season in Doha playing the final. We will see.

Q. You knew him in Spain?

RAFAEL NADAL: When he was in Spain, I never practice with him. He was in Barcelona and I live in

Mallorca all the time. Different places.

Q. How much more confident are you having played like that compared to Thursday night?

RAFAEL NADAL: I am improving, no? I tell last night I finish with very good feelings in the fourth set. I play my best tennis in the season, and today improve the tennis. I play may best today for sure all the time. I feel very comfortable with my forehand, with my serve, with my backhand, too. Today maybe I played a very complete match. That's it. I am very happy because if I continuing play like this, like today, I have a chance for a win, for a winner's match. I can lose too, but I have chance to win.

Q. Are you peaking at the right time?

RAFAEL NADAL: From this year?

Q. Yes.

RAFAEL NADAL: For sure, yeah, hundred percent.

Q. Do you feel physically 100% now?

RAFAEL NADAL: Yeah, for sure. Before the match was a little bit tired, because last match, last night, I have a difficult match, and I don't have too much time. I finish very late. I was sleeping at 5:30, 6:00 in the morning. Just have one day and a little bit more.

But, well, today was not very long match. That's important. For Monday, I going to have hundred percent, for sure.

Q. You don't feel the injury any more?

RAFAEL NADAL: No, I don't feel nothing. Thank you.

Q. You have won many titles as a young player, have lived with the pressure of being No. 2. You've seen in England on your visits what happens to English players under expectation. The pressure that Murray is under, is it the same as yours, or do you see it as different?

RAFAEL NADAL: Oh, well, the pressure, everyone have his pressure, no? I am No. 2, but maybe he wants to be the No. 2 or No. 1, no? I am No. 2 right now. But I have my pressure because I want to continue being No. 2, and he have the pressure for come to No. 2. That's it.

I want to enjoy when I am on court. Now I am -- I feel with a good feeling when playing tennis. When you are playing well and you are in third round, fourth round in Australia, you have to be happy and play. For sure I want to win and I have pressure, but everyone have the same.

Q. Is Murray one of the players that you think in years to come will be one of your great rivals?

RAFAEL NADAL: Well, I don't know, no? I say he's very good player. He can be one of the best players in the world. He is one of the best players of the world right now, no? But he can continuing like this and win Grand Slams, win very good titles. That's it. I don't know if in three years, four years I going to be in the top five. But you never know in the future, no? So for sure he has a very good potential. But is coming very good players, too, no? Young players, new generation, still very good generation: Nalbandian, Hewitt, Roddick, Federer, Davydenko, Blake, Robredo. Every player is there and everyone wants to win because Federer is not old, Roddick is not old, Blake is not old, too. Robredo, Davydenko, every player is maximum 26. So everyone have the chance.

Q. After you won the French Open this year, people were surprised you haven't won since. Coming into 2007, is there any reason why you didn't quite go on in the second half of last season?

RAFAEL NADAL: Well, I know every player in the tour knows how difficult is win a title, no? I don't know. Ferrero was four years maybe playing the Masters Cup, or three. He has 11 titles. Moya, I don't know, a lot of years playing the tour, five Masters Cup, one of the best players of the world every year. He has maybe 19 titles. You know how difficult is win the title, no? I play very bad -- me, in my opinion, I play very bad in Toronto, Cincinnati, the first two Masters Series of the second half of the season. After I play a very good US Open. I play a good US Open. I have a very good chance for be in the semifinals. I lost against Youzhny. Youzhny was playing very good. I play very good in Madrid. Lost against Berdych, was playing a very good match. I lost the semifinals of Shanghai against the best, Federer. That's it. I don't play too much tournaments, just play six tournaments. I have my chance in three.

Q. Murray has made a habit of beating Spanish players. He beat Martin, then Verdasco. Have you spoken to either of them since they played the matches?

RAFAEL NADAL: We will see. I have chances -- more chances to lose than to win. I don't know. Every match is different. Every player is different. No one Spanish player is the same. I don't know. For sure he has the chance. If he win today, he has a chance for beat me and arrive to the final and win the tournament because he's very good player. But I will try my best.

Q. What about Chela?

RAFAEL NADAL: If it Chela, going to be tough match, too. Chela is a veteran player. He has good experience in all surfaces. Going to be tough, too.

Montreal Masters

August 8, 2007

Q. How was it to play Marat Safin for the first time?

RAFAEL NADAL: Yeah, was tough, no? I start playing very well in the beginning and, yeah, I have some mistakes, and he start to play more aggressive. So, yes, is special feeling, no?

Marat is, well, very aggressive play. He can do always everything. And, well, you are all the match with tension, no, because if he's playing good, is impossible, no?

Q. What were you thinking when it was hard for you to break in the first set? Did you think you might lose the match?

RAFAEL NADAL: Well, I wasn't thinking lose the match, no. I just think about the moment and every point, no? If I lose the first set, the match will be complicate, no?
But, well, the match is long and I fight for sure for every point, no? But, well, he has two set points, so was very close first set.

Q. Did you have a particular strategy? Marat seemed to think you were waiting for him to make mistakes rather than going for shots.

RAFAEL NADAL: Well, I worried about me today, no? First round is difficult have special tactic. I just think about me, think about try to play as good as possible because, yes, you never know what's going on.

Is the first round. Is the first match on hard after long time without playing on grass and on clay. Is difficult play well, no? Just try to play good, no?

Q. How comfortable are you playing in Montréal?

RAFAEL NADAL: Right now I have seven match in a row without losing here, so good, no (smiling)?

2005, I play very well, very good tournament - all matches. Today is difficult play very good because Marat is touching the ball with unbelievable power every time, no? But I am there, I fight. In the end I can win, no?

Yes, I know I have to improve something for tomorrow. I have to improve the serve. I have to improve play little bit more aggressive with the forehand. And that's it, no? I know that's important for try to win tomorrow. I'm going to work on that tomorrow morning.

Q. How many players have you played who hit the ball as hard as Marat does?

RAFAEL NADAL: Well, today a lot of players hit the ball very hard, no? But like Marat, not much.

Q. What are you thinking when Marat throws his racquet?

RAFAEL NADAL: Nothing.

Q. Happy?

RAFAEL NADAL: Happy, me?

Q. He's getting frustrated.

RAFAEL NADAL: No feelings, no.

Q. Doesn't bother you?

RAFAEL NADAL: No.

Q. Are you comfortable with the surface, because you seem to slide a little bit?

RAFAEL NADAL: Yes, is normal hard surface. Is fast, is one of the fastest courts in the tour. But I prefer little bit faster. Is fine.

Q. Did you try playing more on his forehand or his backhand?

RAFAEL NADAL: If I try to play?

Q. Did you try more to his forehand or his backhand?

RAFAEL NADAL: Against Safin?

Q. Yes.

RAFAEL NADAL: Well, I change. All depends of the point because Marat -- I explain. If I can, I change to the forehand. Was good, because is important shot for me, no? But if not, I just try to play as long as possible to the backhand.
If I play short, I know Marat, he kill me, no? He has all shots: the cross, down the line.

Q. We asked you about Safin throwing his racquet. When was the last time you threw your racquet?

RAFAEL NADAL: Never, no? I never put the racquet. Well, today I put the racquet one time there like this, but not for angry. I wasn't angry, no? I it was just very nice point. I never put the racquet on the floor, no.

Q. Do you think you can make it to No. 1?

RAFAEL NADAL: If I going to be the No. 1? You never know, no? You never know, especially if Federer is the No. 1. If Federer is continuing play like this, going to be not soon.

Well, this year I am No. 1 in the race. I have some different points. I gonna be the No. 1 for one more week because I have (speaking in Spanish.)

THE INTERPRETER: He's got enough points to continue to be the race leader at least one more week, but he doesn't have enough points to continue to be the leader. He knows that Roger is the favorite till the end of the year because this is his favorite surface.

RAFAEL NADAL: So I am with calm. I just try to play my best, continue improving my game, no? I am young. Try to work every day for if I have the chance any day.

THE INTERPRETER: To take the opportunity, to take the chance.

Rome Masters

May 11, 2007

After defeating Novak Djokovic in QF

Q. You must be very, very happy about your performance today.

RAFAEL NADAL: I am very happy, yes. I play my best level for sure. Very, very nice match. Playing all time 100% every point. So Djokovic is very, very good player. I think he wasn't play bad match today, no?

He serve very good in the breakpoints. Unbelievable. Every time he beat me with the serve. But finally I play all the time very regular, and that's decisive in the game.

Q. Was it important for you not to lose twice, because you had lost the last time?

RAFAEL NADAL: For me important is be in semifinals. That's the most important thing for me. I don't know. If I loss twice against Djokovic, well, he's a great player. If against one player it can happen, it is against him.

Q. You watch the Davydenko match today?

RAFAEL NADAL: Yes. I saw the match. He was playing very, very good tennis, very good rhythm all time. Playing very hard with all sides. So it's going to be very tough match because Tommy today was playing very good level and he can't win.

Q. Your levels are so high all the time. Was there anything today specifically you were very happy with in your game?

RAFAEL NADAL: Well, I ran very good. I serve good sometimes. And important is with my forehand. When I have my forehand I can have the control of the point, so that's very important for me. Because for my confidence important when I touch my forehand feel I am doing something, no? So now I have a very good feelings on my game, on the backhand, too. Important too though when I was running. The slice working very good today.
So everything I play with all shots, so for me it's very -- perfect match.

Rafael Nadal comments on Tiger Woods controversy at Davis Cup final Dec. 2009 in Barcelona, Spain

Q. Rafael, it's been a very difficult week for Tiger Woods. I was wondering what your reaction is to the news about Tiger Woods? As an international athlete known around the world, you go to parties,

there's a lot of temptations, are you surprised someone who we regard on a pedestal can fall into these temptations?

RAFAEL NADAL: I am surprised that you talk about that.

Q. Everybody is talking about it.

RAFAEL NADAL: That's my surprise. Everybody can have his privacy life. We are nobody to talk about his privacy life, no? He don't has to say, explain to nobody about what he's doing in his private life. That's my think. I think he's a big champion and we have to respect his private life.

Miami Masters

March 29, 2015

After losing in three sets in the second round to Fernando Verdasco

Q. It seemed you found a way in the second set, and then it totally went away in the third. What was the sensation today? How can you explain how it went?

RAFAEL NADAL: No, in general, I played some good games at the beginning, bad games at the end of the second set; some good games on the second; not bad at the beginning of the third.

But he played well the third, so he deserved to win more than me without any doubt tonight. Just congratulate him for the victory.

Q. Do you feel that you haven't been able to build up much momentum this season?

RAFAEL NADAL: It's not the question of tennis. The thing is the question of being enough relaxed to play well on court. Something that if I tell you one month ago or one month and a half ago I didn't have the game.

Today my game in general improved since a month and a half. But at the same time, still playing with too much nerves for a lot of moments, in important moments, still playing with a little bit of anxious on that moments.

For example, in the 4-3 in the first set, and then in the 5-4, 30-Love. Something that didn't happen a lot during my career. I have been able to be under control, control my emotions during, let's say, 90%, 95% of my matches of my career, something that today is being tougher to be under self-control.

But I'm gonna fix it. I don't know if in one week, in six months, or in one year, but I'm gonna do it.

Q. You obviously had quite a few issues last year. I think your wrist, your back, and the appendicitis. I'm just wondering if you're finding it as easy to trust your body perhaps after those physical problems last year.

RAFAEL NADAL: No. The physical problems are past. I am on competition. I'm playing weeks in a row. Is not an excuse.

What happened last year, yes, the first weeks of the season obviously all the problems that I had didn't help, but talked enough about these kind of things. Is different story today.

As I said before, feeling much more comfortable in my tennis, practicing well, much better than in Australia, much best than Rio de Janeiro and Buenos Aires. But still playing on competition, you know, feeling more tired than usual, feeling that I don't have this self-confidence that when I hit the ball I gonna hit the ball where I want to hit the ball, to go for the ball running and knowing that my position will be the right one.
All these are small things that are difficult to explain. One of the tougher things have been fixed, that is the game, in my opinion. Now I need to fix again the nerves, the self-control on court. That's another issue.

Is not a tough issue to fix, but I gonna keep trying. I am trying my best. I am practicing with the right attitude, I think. I arrive in an important part of the season for me. I didn't want arrive to that part of the season with that loss of today, obviously, but that part of the season arrives.

It's the next for me, and I am excited. I am enough motivated to keep working hard, and that's what I gonna do. The tournaments that are coming are tournaments that are historically good tournaments for my game, good tournaments for my confidence.

Is true if I'm not able to control all these things, I don't gonna to have the possibility to compete well and have have success on that events. But still with confidence that I can do it.

Q. I think it's very interesting you're talking about nerves and self-control. I mean, you seem like you have won so many big matches in your career that you always seem to have that confidence and that swagger about you. Why do you think this has happened? When did you start feeling that way?

RAFAEL NADAL: It happened when I came back. Beginning of the season I am playing with, you know, all these feelings that for moments are new. You know, I am not saying that didn't happen in the past because happened, but happened for a very small --for one point, two points.

Happened, and then (snapping fingers) I'm able to say, Okay, I am here. But now, for example, happened for, you know, 3-All break point, more or less easy forehand. That was a very important point for me, but shouldn't be that important, you know. I lost that point, and then affects to the next game. I am playing with the next game with more nerves. Then I had the break back, 30-Love, and then again I miss a forehand. That created me doubts again.

So a little bit on and off, on and off too much. That's something that didn't happen in the past, no?

I'm trying to be honest. I am saying the things that I feel today. But at the same time, I tell you that I have been able to able to change a lot of situations, a lot of negative situations in my career, and I want to do it again. Gonna work to do it again. I am confident that I can do it. I don't know if I gonna do it, but I hope I can.

Q. Have you ever felt this kind of nervousness or lack of self-confidence before in your career?

RAFAEL NADAL: I said yes. I said before yes. But not for, let's say, four games in a row, no? Happened for two points and then I was able to be back and to forget about that two mistakes. Now takes a little bit more time.

For example, I was able to be back on the match today, but between 5-3, 4-3, and 2-1, break point for him, I was not there, you know. And I was not there not because I didn't want to be there, no? Because I was with negative attitude being there.

Because I was playing with too much nerves. I was anxious on court. It's not the thing that, you know-- well, is not like maybe some players happen that four games because they lost the concentration and they didn't have the right attitude there. Is not my case, no? Is not my case.

I wanted to be there. I tried in every point, but I was not able to relax myself, calm myself, say I'm going to play my tennis now.

Q. As this is a problem in your head, if you like, have you thought about consulting a sports psychologist? Many top golfers say the sports psychologists were very, very important in recapturing their game and getting over these problems. Are you thinking about doing that?

RAFAEL NADAL: Seriously, I said a lot of times in my career that tennis is not a big deal in life. (Smiling.) You know, medical treatment you need when you have problems. Outside of the tennis world when you have some problems in your life, is a good help that you visit a professional that can help you to improve your quality of life.

Is sport, is game. That's not that much important. But I don't know. I didn't think about. Is something that I need to fix for myself and with my team. I need the help of my team, too.

But especially I need the help of myself. That's what I am trying to do. Nobody gonna change the situation for you. You have to know that you have a problem and you have to know that you have to improve that. You have to change that. I gonna keep working on it.

Hopefully the clay helps. Is obvious that if I am able to win my matches on clay, to feel my game confident there, then the doubts are less.

Thanks to Asap Sports for press conference transcripts.

Chapter 4: ATP Players Discuss Rafael Nadal in Press Conference Interviews

(Photo by Scoop Malinowski.)

Andre Agassi discusses Rafa Nadal at 2004 Madrid Masters

Q. What do you think about the Spanish player Rafael Nadal? We don't know if he's going to be ready to play against you because he's a bit injured, but what do you think about him?

ANDRE AGASSI: He's ready to play against anybody. He's a great talent. Watching him play is a lot of fun. I haven't had the opportunity to play against him or to practice against him. But very strong player. You never know what somebody's game is like until you play them yourself. I certainly enjoy watching him.

Roger Federer discusses Nadal before their first match in Miami Masters 2004:

Q. What is your scouting report on Rafael Nadal?

ROGER FEDERER: Luckily, I played him in doubles last week so I know a little bit more about his game than I would have. So at least I don't have to see him play anymore because I know how he plays now, and I'm looking forward. It's gonna be a good match. He's definitely one of the guys that will be around in the future.

Q. His scouting report, if he had to play you, was if he plays as well as he's capable of playing and you have a bad day, he can win. Otherwise, he says, he loses. What is your reaction to that?

ROGER FEDERER: Well, I mean, I guess he wants to take some pressure off himself, which is kind of normal. Because maybe people expect already too much of him. I don't know, people expect him maybe to beat me on a good day, which I think is totally possible. But he's right, he should push it away from him. Tomorrow he's definitely got a chance. Today wasn't my best, and I got to improve.

Lleyton Hewitt talking about Rafael Nadal before their first match at 2004 Australian Open.

Q. Nadal, your next opponent, what do you know about him?

LLEYTON HEWITT: Very talented young player. Yeah, what I've heard, what I've seen - little bits I've seen - he's a hell of a prospect coming up. It's going to be a tough match. I've got to go up to another level, I think. I look forward to the challenge, though.

Q. There's a bit of talk about him. Is there talk amongst the players about him coming up?

LLEYTON HEWITT: Yeah, I think so. Probably more so -- you know, I probably heard a little more from the media, whatever, maybe last year sometime when he had some pretty good wins over Moya and I think Costa maybe on clay, as well. So clay's his number one surface at the moment. But he had a pretty good run at Wimbledon. I watched a couple of his matches there on TV. He played pretty well on grass, for his first time on grass. He seems like he's got a really good head on him, as well. He's handled the expectation and the pressures very well. You know, he's just one of the next Spaniards coming up. There's a lot of them.

***

Hewitt talking about Nadal after the 2004 Australian Open match.

Q. You were saying out there that you expect a tough match. Was it even tougher than you thought, the young boy tonight?

LLEYTON HEWITT: Yeah. I seen a little bit of his second-round match. He played a lot better tonight than he did in that second-round match, I tell you. He could have very easily been down two sets to one in that match against Ascione, I think, the French bloke. And it wasn't until the other guy started getting a few cramps that he actually got on top of him. He really went up another couple of levels tonight. Yeah, he's a great player. As I said before, you know, all the good stuff you've heard and seen in the past, you know, he's going to be very good in a couple of years.

***

Hewitt talking about Nadal before their 2005 Australian Open match.

Q. Your thoughts on your next match, Nadal?

LLEYTON HEWITT: Yeah, doesn't get any easier. Just another step up, I guess. Yeah, he was obviously a little bit fortunate a couple of days ago to get out of that match against Youzhny. But then tonight, from all accounts, you know, he's destroyed a guy that, you know, he probably should destroy, as well. It's going to be a tough match. He's a worthy opponent, playing Round of 16 in a Grand Slam, on any surface, I think. And he's hungry, he really is. You know, he loves going out there, playing big matches. That's something that I really respect in, you know, a young guy like him, you know, the way that he handles the situation. He played Roddick at the US Open in a night match, and I thought he handled himself really well in that situation. Davis Cup final in Spain, that's not an easy thing to do, to play in a final at such a young age. He handled it incredibly well. I don't think the situation is going to worry him too much. Plus, we also had a tough match here last year in the third round so...

Q. What is his potential? Is he going to be up there with you top guys pretty soon?

LLEYTON HEWITT: I think so. He's been -- at least last year, I think the year before, he might have been injured for the French Open or a lot of the clay court season. He's a lot better player than whatever his ranking is, to not be seeded. He's good on all surfaces. As I said, he's hungry, he's intense, he's competitive, he's all of that, and he's good for the game. I'll be very surprised if he didn't win the French Open one day.

I've looked at a lot of Nadal's matches over the last couple years. The big matches don't worry him. He's that kind of kid. He's like me when I was 16, 17, playing Andre Agassi in front of your home crowd.

That was awesome for me. Very similar to him. He didn't take a step back against Roddick at the US Open, maybe the second round they played. He took it to him. Obviously, Andy was too good and too powerful at the time. But, yeah, he doesn't step back for anyone.

Montreal Masters

August 14, 2005

Andre Agassi after losing final to Nadal

Q. You said you'd have the best seat in the house. I'm curious as to your impressions of the young man.

ANDRE AGASSI: Well, he has a difficult game. It's certainly easy to see why he's won so many matches. He does a lot of things really well. Just a great mover on the court. Gets good power from very stretched positions so you're never quite sure if you have complete control of the point. I found his serve more awkward than I was anticipating because if you don't hit a good return, he immediately gets on the offense. That's a sign of a great player: somebody who can play good defense, but also when they get ahold of a point, they don't let go of it. He's one of those guys that if he gets ahold of a point, he's not going to let go of it. It puts more pressure on you to hit a quality return, and it moves a little bit. I felt like today that was a big difference. I wasn't getting neutral enough right off his serve. That surprised me a little bit.

Q. Did your game plan change at all after the rain delay? Looked like in the second set you were maybe coming into the net a little more.

ANDRE AGASSI: I think it was a product of just playing a set against him. I mean, we never even hit balls together. So you haven't even felt what his ball does, let alone what his best shots are. And after the rain delay, I certainly had a good feel for what his ball was going to do, which allowed me to be a little bit more convicted on my shots. Yeah, so it changed a little bit.

Q. We know you like to take the ball pretty early. It looked like you were a little bit closer up to the baseline at the start of the match on Nadal's serve, a little bit further back towards the end. Is that a good assessment?

ANDRE AGASSI: Yeah, that is a good assessment. That was the case. I thought -- you know, you watch him on TV, it looks like he just rolls that serve in. It looks like you should be able to hit it pretty effectively. But it is a lefty action with sort of a slice sometimes kick to it. So the ball's moving around a bit. If you don't hit it square, you leave anything hanging, and that's where he's really dangerous. So it's not so much that you can't stand up on the serve as much as if you don't hit it perfectly, you're going to pay for that. And I felt like I wasn't getting into enough points on his serve, so I drifted back to give myself a chance just to hit a quality cut and get into the point, which turned out to be pretty necessary. You know, the ball's jumping out there. The way he hits it, it's even jumping that much more.

Q. What are your impressions of getting two standing ovations during a match? Pretty special, no?

ANDRE AGASSI: Yeah, yeah, some great, warm expressions of appreciation out there. Man, I just take those moments in more now than I ever have. It was pretty special. It's been a lot of years I've been coming here, so that just motivates me to keep trying.

Q. He broke your serve I think twice in that third set. Obviously, that's somewhere you don't want to go.

ANDRE AGASSI: Yeah, the 3-1 game, I mean, that's the game that I sort of consider to be the worst game of the match for me. We had a long first point for me to go up 15-Love. He took a lot of time to recover from that point when I was waiting to serve. I was trying to get Lars to tell him he has to play at my pace. So I lost concentration there a little bit. Immediately threw a double-fault in, then I made a quick error. All of a sudden, after a long point I won with him sort of breathing hard, he had 50 seconds in between those two points alone to recover, and I was serving 15-30. You know, I get it back to 30-40 and dump a forehand I never should have missed. That game was the nail in the coffin.

Q. Would you like to see that enforced more from the chair umpires, considering you seem to keep

yourself in such good shape on the tour?

ANDRE AGASSI: I got to believe he knows the rules. I was always under the impression that you sort of have to play to the server's pace. Rafael is very a practical, calculated, sort of methodical player. He takes his time. It's great to see somebody have that sense about themselves at such a young age, where they take their time and they execute. He should have the right to do that. But there's also a need to play to the server's pace. I'm not sure where the subtleties fall on that particular rule. I just felt like if the server can play at a certain pace, so can the returner. That's certainly what I've always tried to hold myself to. But we might be splitting hairs there when it comes to how that's interpreted.

Q. Can you compare him to other players in terms of his quickness?

ANDRE AGASSI: You know, there's so many different ways to assess speed. You got guys that are tremendously fast, but they only use their speed defensively, then you really don't care about how fast they are because they're only going to have to run more. You got other guys that can use their speed offensively, but if you get them on the defense they can't hurt you on the stretch, so you can take a point over early and they can be fast but never turn a point around. Nadal has the ability to run as fast as the best of 'em, but on the stretch actually hurt you. You know, he can transition those points into offense. That makes you sort of walk on egg shells. He draws out errors that I think normally you wouldn't make against any other player, which is a credit to the way he plays the game.

Q. When you came in on the Pro Tour 17, 18 years ago, they nicknamed you "the kid." Do you see yourself in this new kid on the block?

ANDRE AGASSI: No, I don't see myself. He's a unique person to himself. I mean, everybody is.

ROME MASTERS

May 11, 2007

Novak Djokovic

Q. Just how good is Rafa at the moment? He seems maybe better than ever.

NOVAK DJOKOVIC: Well, certainly I knew that he's the best player in the world on this surface before the match, and I was aware of that.

What I was trying to do is to go out there and be aggressive, but in the same time try to be patient, which is very difficult. Because the balls you don't get back on the hard courts you get back on the clay.

He's really feeling comfortable on this surface, but I'm really satisfied with the way I played today. Just I have time to improve.

Q. Have you learned much from today's match about how you would play him next time on clay?

NOVAK DJOKOVIC: Yeah, I always learn some new things when I play against the best players in the world. Every match is a new experience.

Yes, today I've seen, you know, what I need to improve on and what I need to do so I can play better in the next match and maybe try to win.

Of course, you know, it's very difficult to play him on this surface. It's the surface he prefers. But, you know, I'll really do my best and then practice and try to beat him on the clay if I have the next chance.

In this moment I'm really happy the way I play on clay. Even today's performance was really good. He was better, and that's all really. I won last week tournament in Estoril. Won two very difficult matches here before Nadal, and playing with a lot of confidence. Helps me a lot.

Q. You tried to play a lot of dropshots. Did you feel that this was the right tactic against him?

NOVAK DJOKOVIC: It's one of the things, yes. To try to, you know, put him out of the comfort zone. You got to try to do something else, and you got to be physically really hundred percent ready.

Q. Were you worried at all today having won Estoril and the tough matches here the physical part of it? You seemed to hold up physically. Were you worried you might not be able to?

NOVAK DJOKOVIC: I worked a lot after Monte-Carlo tournament, the week after, and as well in Estoril I worked a lot on physical preparation, because I want to be physically ready for the Rome, Hamburg, and especially Roland Garros.

I think here I had the very difficult matches, but today I felt pretty good on the court and I was running a lot. You know, we had long points, long games, so I'm really happy with the way I feel now. I'm not too tired, you know.

So not too exhausted, and that's a positive thing because that was the goal at the start of the clay court season: To prepare for the major tournaments.

Q. What do you think you should improve in your playing for to be closer to him, to Roger or Nadal?

NOVAK DJOKOVIC: I'm not really in a hurry anywhere. I'm trying to practice and to focus on my career. And I know that I need a lot of experience and a lot of things to improve on so I can get to the place I want to be: The best player in the world.

There is time. I'm only twenty years old this year. I hope my career will be ten to fifteen more years long. You know, what I will try to do is to improve more on the volleys so I can, you know, use my opportunities. Because I have pretty good groundstrokes from the baseline, pretty powerful and aggressive, but I need

to go more to the net so I can use those opportunities, and of course serve consistency.
There is a lot of things. You cannot play perfect.
There is always things you can improve on.

Q. You play well on all surfaces. Where do you rate clay?

NOVAK DJOKOVIC: I think I prefer mostly hard court. You know, clay is one of the surface I play well on as well. You know, of course I lost straight sets against a player who didn't lose close to 18 matches in a row, so I'm not really down because of it.
You know, I still have confidence and I still think that I'm one of the best players in the world on this surface as well.

Q. We could watch you and see that you see an opening, and that opening against most players you'll hit a winner into. What goes through your mind when you see the opening with him and it seems like so often he can get them?

NOVAK DJOKOVIC: As I said, with the balls you make winner on hard court against him or some other players, and here you get the ball back. Here the conditions, the courts are pretty fast, so it should be better for the other players to play against him.
But it seems like he likes it as well. He can play on all kinds of surfaces. He proved that in Wimbledon last year. I'm aggressive type, you know, of the player. I like to make winners, and sometimes I make a lot of unforced errors because of that. But these are some

things that I need to improve on: Consistency and more patient.

Q. On clay this year do you think he's got further away from everyone compared to last year?

NOVAK DJOKOVIC: He's playing really fantastic tennis. In Monte-Carlo he didn't lose a set. Nobody had a chance against him. Barcelona as well and here as well. He's playing really impressive, so he's getting away.

Rome Masters

May 12, 2007

Nikolay Davydenko

Q. Is there anything you could have done better today?

NIKOLAY DAVYDENKO: For me, yeah, like today was I think from my opinion was good, like start to play tennis of clay court season and to prove something against Nadal.

How against him I need to play most, you know, because I need to play like against -- like against another guy like different players you need to play different games, you need to play different tennis. So today was a little bit different. And it was, yeah, Nadal fighting every ball to try to do the same. But I see he have always trouble. It was good way what I did in play against him.

Q. What do you think about the difference at the end?

NIKOLAY DAVYDENKO: I think like after 4-3 it's like, you know, it was already tough match. It's was like pretty tough to keep running, right, left, and he start -- you know, like my brother say I start to play, right, left and he move already with, you know, like starting to play a little bit harder from backhand and from one hand. Forehand he start to make more quick to me to the backhand cross. After three hours it's pretty tough running there and hitting ball from the backhand. I need to have good control also to play long line or very good cross, because before I was playing like control ball and hitting ball always. Get top spin, good to the backhand or long line across. And already in the third set you just try to hit back ball and just control, no mistake. That's pretty tough. And he just see already I am tired and he try to move me more, like to make more kick, more top spin. Move me more and more, and that's why I was completely ... cannot ... he makes winners in this point.

Q. You must feel a lot more confident about beating him next time you play.

NIKOLAY DAVYDENKO: It's good. Today was good match. Like every match for me like most of two hours and today was three hours. I don't know, maybe next time play against him five hours. But it's good like practicing, because I hit so many balls from forehand and backhand, you know, like good confidence. Like already I play already many matches and play long matches and, okay, physically maybe it's pretty tough because always you need to be ready for the next day. But it's good I did good fitness here for every day and I help my confidence and everything be okay, recovery for the Hamburg tournament. I try to be there already physically and mentally good to prepare and also important to be ready Roland Garros.

Q. Compared to last year, 2006 when you lost to Roger in the Australian Open, it was a very, very good match. How are your feelings now losing to a very good player, same as Rafa and Roger last year?

NIKOLAY DAVYDENKO: I think it's like -- for me, most -- I losing not to tennis, more physically because I'm tired, and then I lose concentration. This point, if I start to play like some point and I do mistake because you already tired and you cannot have such good concentration with ball and you try to hit ball to the line and you do mistake or you hit ball out. That's how my body was, like my shoulder is already tired to hit the same like before, like first set or last set. It's pretty tough. And I was like not like Nadal physically strong -- I need to improve I think more physically. If I have more good physically I can finish better and better. My tennis right now I have not so bad because today against Nadal I play good. The only problem I think was not mental, it's physically. Because sometimes

I'm already like tired and losing concentration and do mistake only for this reason.

Q. You feel he was not tired? Do you feel that he was not tired?

NIKOLAY DAVYDENKO: I don't know. Like it's tough to say because he running so far and always I make like -- he try to run to every ball. That's was in three hours or three hours and thirty minutes we play already. In the first set I do dropshot volley and he try to run to come back and I was surprised. For me I don't want to run already for his ball and he try to come back. He try to, you know, every ball to catch. It's amazing.   I think he's physically, you know, great.

Q. Set point in the first set, the dropshot, was that just --

NIKOLAY DAVYDENKO: Yeah, that was also terrible for me. It was not tough. I was running and I have control with the ball, but I don't know why I put the net. But normally if I put in the court Nadal can run and I have no chance to do something. Because I'm already -- I need to make winners with last ball. It was only last chance what I need to, but I try to make dropshot cross, and net. But bad luck. I have already set point there, but...

And how many set point I have in the tiebreak or before in the second set?

Q. Can you imagine Nadal not losing a single match on clay this year?

NIKOLAY DAVYDENKO: We'll see. It's coming, more tournaments: Roland Garros still. He's, yeah, I don't know if -- it's not like -- I don't know how to say. He's physically strong, yeah. If like he is running like today three hours and like in Roland Garros it's five-set match. We just play three sets. If he running five sets like this in five hours, yeah, then I don't know.

But I never see some guy running five hours like first set and last set. But tennis-wise, I don't think he's the best because I was playing now and I was surprising. From baseline I also play better, and he just he have good forehand from one hand. He play very good kick and make winners from only one side. But from the backhand he's normal. That's was always I try to do to play there and just to change some games. He was in trouble in this time.

Q. How would you have felt if you had to play tomorrow against (Fernando) González? And how do you think Rafa will feel after such a tough match today?

NIKOLAY DAVYDENKO: It's like how will González play tomorrow, because Nadal do the same game always. So I don't know. If González play fast I think for Nadal most easy. Because against Nadal, like how you say, if I try to play faster he running more faster and to bring ball back fast. And you know, it's difficult then to control. If you play against a little bit slow and easy he cannot push ball from the backhand. He try to do something and he can't. Then I have time to prepare for the next ball and I know what I need to do then. If I try to make some winners, fast to play, he running fast and make great top spin today for the baseline, and I have no chance the next time. That's why I know what González play. He stay also behind, like far from the baseline and hitting balls pretty fast. We'll see tomorrow.

Rome Masters

May 13, 2007

Fernando Gonzalez

Q. 40-15 in the first game. Was that disturbing to let that get by?

FERNANDO GONZÁLEZ: Maybe, because I lost the match, but he was playing really good. I mean, it's tough when you play against a guy that feel very comfortable on the court and you don't feel really good, especially playing against him. Everything can be different, but there is nothing that I can do now.

Q. Can you talk about how different it is to play Nadal on clay than like another surface, like the Australian Open.

FERNANDO GONZÁLEZ: Clay is his best surface

and hard court is maybe my best surface. Tennis you can play in different surfaces, and sometimes the ball flies a lot and sometimes it's slow. It's different. In tennis it's very competitive and every day different. But, I mean, we're playing on clay now and I have to try to keep improving. This was a good week for me, especially if you go back one or two weeks and I was playing really bad on this surface.

Q. Is anybody every going to beat this guy on clay?

FERNANDO GONZÁLEZ: Hopefully. It's boring if he's winning every clay court tournament. But he's, I mean, he's very -- I mean, his shots, he try to play very high and deep, and it's tough because he's in good shape and he can be hours playing there. That's why today I tried to go for it, tried to win the match. I cannot wait on this kind of surface.

Q. Were you hoping he might be tired after yesterday's match?

FERNANDO GONZÁLEZ: Not really, because, I mean, he can run hours and come back the next day. So, no, no. I never expect that, but I was happy that they played three hours yesterday.

Q. You said you didn't play too well. Do you have any reason for it, why you weren't at your best today?

FERNANDO GONZÁLEZ: I think the reason was him. It's easy to say I didn't play good or I play bad or my serve didn't work. I mean, maybe you have another reason, but the most important is your opponent. Sometimes he makes you play where you don't want to play.
I tried to attack him all the time, tried to play very close to the baseline to try to make my opportunity to go into the net, and I couldn't do. So that was my plan for today.

Q. Say you're just all the players and you have to beat Nadal on clay. What have you learned from playing him on clay that maybe you would do differently? Is there anything you can see that you might be able to do on clay to have more success?

FERNANDO GONZÁLEZ: There was a little bit wrong with my serve. Tried to -- I mean, try to put more first serve in. Don't try to find the free points, because anyway you have to play long points. But, I mean, he plays good tennis today. I mean, maybe you can take something when he's not playing really good.

Montreal Masters

August 8, 2007

Marat Safin after playing first time vs. Nadal, losing 76 60.

Q. You talked before about matches like this giving you a good indication of where you are, what you need to do. First set was very tight.

MARAT SAFIN: The only thing, if you really start to think, it's just a matter of me missing these kind of matches with such players, level as a Nadal, Federer, top 10 players. It's the only thing, because you don't get to play against them many times because they don't get there.

But with these kind of matches, you improve your tennis actually. After what I saw today, I had my opportunities. I was a little bit nervous at the beginning, but then I start to figure out how to play against him. Just a lot of mistakes, easy mistakes, because probably I had a little bit too much precipitation (sic), going for too much.
But the only thing is just missing these kind of matches, to play more and more and more.

Q. Is it quite encouraging overall?

MARAT SAFIN: Yeah, the second set, we can forget it. But actually the level of tennis, now I know more or less what I have to do, what I have to improve to make my game a little more complete. But definitely I can play against these kind of players and I'm pretty far from letting it go and just keep on working on a few things and things is going to be all right. This match really showed me where I am.

Q. What do you think you need to do?

MARAT SAFIN: Yeah, well, just stick to my game, you know, come a little bit closer to the baseline faster. That's how I play before, that's how I was winning matches. Unfortunately with my injury with the knee, I went a little back, so I had to learn a little bit different type of game because I couldn't play as fast as I used to play. I couldn't move as fast as I need to move.

But now that the knee is okay, I need just to try to play a little bit closer to the line, play a little bit faster.

Q. When you don't play as many matches like that against top 10 players, do you sort of forget a little bit of what you need to do?

MARAT SAFIN: Of course, because you want so badly, you see opportunities. I can see the match, I can read what was going on; the only thing I need to do is maybe go for it sometimes. I stayed on the baseline, was going for it on the wrong shots. So these kind of things made the score 7-6, 6-Love.

If I would win the first set, then it's going to be a different ballgame because he would be a little bit nervous and then I have a little bit more confidence, the whole picture change.

Q. After playing him now, would you play him differently if you played him again?

MARAT SAFIN: No, the same way. I have to use my power and be a little bit smarter, maybe wait for an extra ball. But it was a little bit too windy for me today, so kind of a lot of miss-hits. But otherwise it was a pretty good match because it's pretty comfortable for me to play against him because he leaves the ball too high up, so for me it's easy to play. He doesn't play too fast, as fast as I thought he was going to play.

So I expect a little bit different game plan from him and I was a little bit surprised so I didn't really -- I was -- I thought it was going to be a different game from him.

Q. Did you expect more power?

MARAT SAFIN: I expected more power. I expected the game is going to be faster, the level of the game would be a little bit faster and more intense. He let me play for basically the whole match.

Q. You were dominating the rallies.

MARAT SAFIN: Yeah, but he's a good (indiscernible). He knew the opportunities. He went for the right one on the set point where I had the first one. He went down the line with the backhand. I think it's pretty good shot. But otherwise he knew what he was doing and he was waiting for me to make mistakes.
Now I know, and for me it's easier to see the picture for next match. I hope is going to be a little bit different.

Miami Masters

April 2, 2009

Juan Martin Del Potro def. Nadal 6-4, 3-6, 7-6

Q. What do you think was the difference today for you? You've never beaten him before, never taken a set off him, I don't think. Why today do you think it turned?

JUAN MARTIN DEL POTRO: Because always I was keep going and keep trying. I beat him with my mind and with my game. When we played long points, I was dominating every time, so that was the key of the last set, of the tiebreak.
But I beat for first time.

Q. Did you come into this match thinking differently about him, or did you just come in the middle of the match and you realized you had a chance?

JUAN MARTIN DEL POTRO: No. I know him since 12 years. We play many times. Sometimes I can play good and sometimes bad, but today I did everything. I served very good, and with my forehand with big confidence. To beat Rafa, you have to be in good shape and every part of your game, and today I did a great job.

Q. Did it feel like Buenos Aires out there, and how much did that help you?

JUAN MARTIN DEL POTRO: Yeah, a lot. There are many Argentinians and Latino, they all support me a lot. They help me too much for this victory.

Q. Rafa did not think that you played unbelievably good. He didn't think it was one of your better matches. He thought he really played terribly? How would you categorize your play tonight?

JUAN MARTIN DEL POTRO: I played unbelievable. I beat the No. 1 of the world. If you don't play unbelievable, you cannot beat him. I'm happy, but tomorrow I will play again, so I have to think in the next match.

Q. It looked like when you were down 2-3 in the tiebreak that you got aggressive and you took the match to him. Did you feel that way?

JUAN MARTIN DEL POTRO: Well, I have a little bit lucky in the tiebreak. But I fight like three hours to be in the tiebreak, so five more points will be to decide to the match, and I was trying until the final. That's was the big thing of the match.

Q. You're down 3-0 at the beginning of the third, two breaks. What are you thinking right then?

JUAN MARTIN DEL POTRO: Well, I start to enjoy the

match, the people, the crowds, the quarterfinals. And I start to play more relaxes and more aggressive, too. Then the match going different. I broke his serve in 3-0, and then 3-2. When I was 5-4, I say, Now I can beat him. That's was a big difference in my mind.

Q. Even when you had three match points and you had the forehand set up, even when you missed that, you still believed?

JUAN MARTIN DEL POTRO: Yeah. Because Rafa did two aces, and then I have my opportunity with my forehand. But sometimes go in and sometimes no. The important is I was fighting until the final, and now I'm happy for the victory.

Q. Is this the biggest moment of your career?

JUAN MARTIN DEL POTRO: Of course.

Thanks to ASAP Sports for press conference transcripts. www.asapsports.com

----

2014 Miami Masters

Novak Djokovic

I think challenges, big challenges that I had in my career changed me in a positive way as a player. Because of Rafa and because of Roger I am what I am today, you know, in a way, because when I reached the No. 3 in the world and won the first Grand Slam title in 2008, the years after that I struggled a lot mentally to overcome the doubts that I had. And all the big matches I lost to these guys was consistent but not winning the big matches, and then they made me understand what I need to do on the court. I worked hard, and, you know, it's paying dividends, I guess, in the last couple of years. You know, obviously it's not easy when you're playing a top rival at the finals of any tournament, but if you want to be the best, you have to beat the best, you know. You have to win against the best players in the world. That's the biggest challenge you can have.

Yes, definitely biggest rivalry I have in my tennis career. It's a great challenge always when I play Rafa on any surface, of course, especially on clay. That is his most preferred surface, his most dominant there. I have had some thrilling matches in last three or four years, and they were decided by few points. It was very few matches that were one- sided, so I knew what to expect from Rafa today. When he fights for trophy, he comes out with a great intensity from the first point, and he wants to make sure he sends the message across the net to his opponent.
That's why at the start I faced the break point, it was quite even, and then making a break obviously gave

me huge sign of relief and I could swing freely and more confidently. So that rivalry that we have is obviously great for the sport. It's great for us. I'm enjoying every single match. Hopefully we can have many more.

Chapter 5: More Facing Rafa Interviews

(Photo by Scoop Malinowski.)

"I think he hates to lose more than anything else."

Leander Paes: "I've played Rafa quite a few times in doubles. Played him in Dubai in the final many, many years ago, when he first came up on the Tour. Played him in Indian Wells a bunch of times, with Lopez. The one thing that stands out is his fierce competitiveness. I think he hates to lose more than anything else. And the way he prepares himself for every match, the way he gets ready for every point, shows how much effort he puts into his tennis. For me, he is one of the champions of the game because of the effort that he puts into his game, and maximizes every opportunity that he gets."

Question: Remember your record vs. Rafa?

Leander Paes: "No idea."

Question: What was the most memorable match you played against Rafa?

Leander Paes: "A few of them. I beat him in the finals of Dubai once. He got me in Palm Springs with Lopez, a really tight, tough match, three sets, late at night. We've had some good battles out there. It would have been very interesting to have played him in singles at some point."

Question: Is Rafa the hardest guy for you to play?

Leander Paes: "I always thought (Andre) Agassi was the hardest guy to play because Andre just had such a complete game. He had a brilliant net game too. And the fact that he could hit drive volleys. The fact that he could come in and mix it up every once in a while - and hit little touch volleys. Rafa's gotten a lot better at that now. His left-handed game definitely makes him more potent out there. So he's definitely one of the toughest ones out there."

Question: Lasting memory or anecdote of Rafa, on or off court, that maybe captures his essence?

Leander Paes: "I think more than anything, his respectfulness on the Tour. The way he's respected the other players of the game. The way he's always respected me in the locker room in the way he talks and communicates. I mean, to me, someone that's a gentleman like that, off the court, makes him an even bigger champion, in my mind."

Paes leads doubles series 3-2

2012 Indian Wells QF Nadal/M.Lopez vs. Paes/Stepanek W 6-3, 7-6

2011 Cincinnati R16 Nadal/M. Lopez vs. Paes/Bhupathi L 4-6, 2-6

2010 Indian Wells R32 Nadal/M. Lopez vs. Paes/Dlouhy W 6-4, 3-6, 10-6

2008 Indian Wells R32 Nadal/Ferrer vs. Paes/Hanley L 3-6, 4-6

2005 Barcelona F Nadal/F. Lopez vs. Paes/Zimonjic L 3-6, 3-6

"He's such a super cool guy."

Andrei Pavel: "Well, I only played him in doubles. Two times. He has one of the fastest arms on the Tour. He's striking the ball so fast, the ball takes so much spin. And the way he moves and the power he puts on the ball is amazing."

Question: Any standout memories of the matches?

Andrei Pavel: "I played once the final of Doha against him. Me and Mikhail Youzhny and we lost to him and Albert Costa. And then I beat him actually, a German guy Alex Waske, we beat him in the final of Barcelona. So I'm 1-1 against him. He's an amazing champion. Good to have a win on him, at least in doubles [smiles]."

Question: Lasting memory or anecdote of Rafa?

Andrei Pavel: "I think he's a super nice guy and he's a bit shy but I know that once in Madrid, friends of mine, they were getting married and they were fans of him and I asked him to just say a couple of words on the phone and he did it so easily, without even blinking. And he's such a super cool guy."

Doubles series tied 1-1

2007 Barcelona F Nadal/B. Salva-Vidal vs. Pavel/Waske L 3-6, 6-7
2005 Doha F Nadal/A. Costa vs. Pavel/Youzhny W 6-3, 4-6, 6-3

"The best moment so far in my career."

Ivan Dodig: "He's always one of the toughest players to play on the court. And he's unbelievable because an important thing for me - he's never giving up and he has the opportunity always to rise the game. If he's going much more to the end, he's always playing the best tennis."

Question: Your most memorable match with Rafa?

Ivan Dodig: "It was in Montreal when I beat him. This was for me, like, the best moment so far in my career. And I was really enjoying."

Question: That was the first time you played him too, right?

Ivan Dodig: "Actually I played with him - I don't know if I played Barcelona first match with him or in Montreal...Montreal was the first time that I played him. And later on we played a couple of more times but he beat me [smiles]."

Question: How were you able to beat Rafa in Montreal? Your memories of this match?

Ivan Dodig: "Yeah, basically it was kind of an incredible match for me. I was a set down and in the second set 3-1 down and then I came back and won the tiebreak 7-6. Then third set I was again 5-3 down. So I came back and was again in the tiebreak. So it was kind of everything kind of come on my side in the important points."

Question: Was there a special tactic that was working?

Ivan Dodig: "I was trying to be just aggressive on

important points. Especially in the end, I was also a little bit lucky. I went for some shots and I made it. So like on match point when I finish with a winner, his backhand felt basically...I was trying to be as much as possible aggressive. And this was working very well."

Question: Was that the best match you ever played on the ATP World Tour?

Ivan Dodig: "The best for sure, yeah."

Question: Lasting memory on or off court of Rafa?

Ivan Dodig: "For me it's not so much for me to say he's a great champion and I like him on the court how well he's playing, as well off the court. And for me I just can say the best memory was that I beat him [smiles]."

Nadal leads series 3-1

2011   Barcelona   Clay   SF   Nadal   6-3, 6-2

2011   Montreal Masters   Hard R32   Dodig   1-6, 7-6, 7-6 (5)

2013   US Open   Hard   R32   Nadal   6-4, 6-3, 6-3

20V4   Barcelona   Clay   R16   Nadal   6-3, 6-3

"He does give you these opportunities to play aggressive."

Ivan Ljubicic: "Rafa is probably mentally the strongest player that we have on the Tour. I'm not equipped enough to talk about historically but you know from him you're going to get absolute maximum when it comes to mental situations. You know that it's important when you're down break point that he's not going to miss the return. You know that if you drop him a short ball, he's going to take care of it. So for him I always felt that it was not as physical as it looked like to play because, as I said, if you drop that short ball he's going to take care of it. He's not the type of player, like maybe Thomas Muster, that would on purpose make points longer and make you more tired. Rafa is the type of player that's going to kill the point, especially if he can. Sometimes he just has more difficulty to kill it when he's playing against better players but he's not the type of player that it's not going to get physical."

"So what is obviously very, very difficult is to deal with the spins that he has. Those spins are unique in tennis. He's obviously lefty, which doesn't help. And the amount of spin when he can put on the ball is unique in the sport in tennis. So definitely, if you haven't played him in a while, it does take some games to kind of get used to those balls and the trajectory of the ball that you're going to get from that you don't get from anybody else."

"And then after, I always felt against him he does give you these opportunities to play aggressive. And if you're playing well and you are aggressive enough and you play good tennis, you do get a chance. He's not the kind of player that is going to kill you. He does start, especially on hard courts, from further back. So he does give you time to swing. He does give you time to maybe unleash your weapons. But if you don't play well, he's the player that you have the least chance to beat."

Question: Your most memorable match with Rafa? Indian Wells?

Ivan Ljubicic: "Well, positively, Indian Wells. Negatively, Madrid final that I think was the most emotional match that I have ever played. I won first two sets - it was best of five back in the day - and I was physically very tired. But not because of the match itself because I had a really, really long three weeks. I was coming from winning Vienna and playing final of Madrid. So I had a lot of tennis behind me. And the crowd got into it. It was unbelievable atmosphere. Obviously, negative for me but he was enjoying it big time. Then I ended up losing 7-6 in the fifth. But it was a very, very memorable match. If course, Indian Wells (I won) 7-6 in the third. Two matches that were the closest between the two of us."

Question: What happened in Indian Wells? You winning that event was quite a surprise at the time.

Ivan Ljubicic: "I had a day off before that semi, which is unusual in Masters 1000. Indian Wells is one of those that you do get that. So I had the time to maybe prepare for that match maybe a little bit better than usual. A lot of the first set I remember it was a little bit windy. And I also felt like he dropped the concentration a little bit. Because he felt like he had the match under control. After that, I start to serve really, really well. So I didn't give him a chance to break me. I managed to break him in the second set. Third set, I was a break up, he broke me back. But he started to feel real uncomfortable, you can kinda see it. And seeing that, obviously my confidence was growing point to point. Then in the tiebreak, I just played the best tiebreak of my career. I won 7-1. Basically hitting all the clean winners. And it was one of the best moments obviously of my career. But not because of the result - and after, winning the tournament - but because of beating Nadal 7-6 in the third and playing the way I played."

Question: Was Rafa the hardest guy for you to play?

Ivan Ljubicic: "No. No, he wasn't. I felt, like I said before, I felt like against him if you play well you do have a chance which I never really felt against Novak or Roger, especially against Roger. I felt like he had many, many ways to stop my game. Novak was, I think, the best returns in the game, by far. He was the only player - he was not only returning my serves a lot but very well. And that was always the big problem for me being the big server. Roger I just felt like he had many, many ways to win the point. And I always felt like whatever I dropped at him, whatever I threw at him, he just found a way to deal with it. And he's definitely the most creative player that I ever played against."

Question: Lasting memory or anecdote of Rafa?
Ivan Ljubicic: "Well, he's a kind of player, he kills

you, in my opinion, more with mentally than physically, as I said in the beginning. He does start with the slow routine. Even before the match, when you walk on the court, you drop your bag down, you take your racquets, you go to the net, wait for the ball toss and you wait for him like sometimes long minutes. Then he does use every opportunity to break your rhythm, even between points. It makes it uncomfortable. And then by doing it, he does extend the match, time-wise, quite a bit. Which, of course, makes it more difficult for aggressive players to play closer to the lines, to play with higher risk. Obviously, the longer the match is, the bigger chance it is for the opponent to start missing. And I think this is definitely one part of the tactics that a lot of people don't realize."

Nadal leads series 7-2

2011 French Open Clay   R16   Nadal 7-5, 6-3, 6-3

2011 Monte Carlo Masters Clay   QF Nadal   6-1, 6-3

2010 Indian Wells Masters   Hard SF   Ljubicic 3-6, 6-4, 7-6(1)

2009 Shanghai Masters   Hard QF   Nadal   3-6, 6-3 Ret.

2009 Monte Carlo Masters   Clay QF Nadal   6-3, 6-3

2006 French Open   Clay SF   Nadal   6-4, 6-2, 7-6(7)

2005 Madrid Masters   Hard F Nadal 3-6, 2-6, 6-3, 6-4, 7-6(3)

2005 Miami Masters   Hard   R16 Nadal   6-4, 6-7(5), 6-3

2005 Doha   Hard QF   Ljubicic 6-2, 6-7(3), 6-3

"He didn't crack a smile once in three days."

Francis Tiafoe: "We hit for three days. And he didn't crack a smile once in those three days. We hit at Roland Garros. Jay Berger contacted him or Toni Nadal contacted...I don't know how that worked. After I lost in the second round French Open, a really tough loss, Jay said I'm hitting with Nadal. I thought he was joking. I have a court with Nadal. We hit. And Nadal liked it, we hit again. And again. And he said, 'Can we keep going?' Because he's really superstitious. I sad, 'Nah, I gotta go.' I had to fly home."

Question: Did anything surprise you about hitting with Nadal live compared to seeing him on TV?

Francis Tiafoe: "Yeah, he's a lot bigger, taller than he looks on TV. And he hits the ball way harder live than on TV."

Question: Did he offer any advice, was he helpful, or was he more locked in?

Francis Tiafoe: "More locked in. Because, obviously, he's trying to win the French Open for almost the hundredth time [smiles]."

"He just laughed...typical Rafa."

Robby Ginepri: "Well, it was very intimidating when I found out I had to play him at the French Open (2014). After a couple of days went by I did kinda swallow that and get my gameplan going. It's almost like you have to put the match on a repeat cycle because he will play the same exact point over and over and over again. You have to hit about eight shots to win one point. So if you're willing to play those points and if you can have the capabilities to play with him, then you can push him. But no one's done that except for (Robin) Soderling the one year. The guy's just a warrior out there, doesn't give you anything free. The way he moves around the ball, his footwork, he sets everything up with his forehand. His movement, the balls, they're very hard to attack."

Question: Hardest player for you to play against?

Robby Ginepri: "On clay, yeah. There's not too many guys out there that can give me fits like he does. He's one of the best, for sure."

Question: Lasting memory or anecdote about Rafa?

Robby Ginepri: "At the French Open, when I played him and I said, after the match (at net handshake), 'I always wanted to play you on clay and thanks for showing me how to do it.' He just laughed. Typical Rafa."

Nadal leads series 2-0

2014 French Open   Clay R128 Nadal 6-0, 6-3, 6-0

2005 Madrid Masters   Hard SF   Nadal 7-5, 7-6(1)

"I got used to his ball after one day."

Stefan Kozlov hit with Nadal at the 2014 Sony Open in Key Biscayne:

"It was one of the craziest feelings I ever had, to be honest. The first couple of minutes I was trying to move my feet as fast as I could and swing as hard as I could. And the balls were just slicing off my string because of the spin. I don't know if everyone felt that before or it's just me. The first five minutes there with Rafa were one of a kind. Then after that, the second day I hit with him, I actually had one of the best practices of my life. So I got used to his ball after one day."

Question: Rafa asked you back for the second day?

Stefan Kozlov: "Yeah, we hit for like four days."

Question: Before his Sony Open semifinal match?

Stefan Kozlov: "Before semifinal and before final."

Question: How did Rafa treat you?

Stefan Kozlov: "He treated me well. We didn't talk too much but we talked a little. He was really nice during the practice, even if I missed I felt like he was really chill about it, really laid back. I didn't feel any pressure hitting with him."

Question: How did you get the opportunity to hit with the ATP number one player in the world?

Stefan Kozlov: "USTA set it up - Jay Berger."

Question: Lasting memory of this experience?

Stefan Kozlov: "It took me like two hours to get into the stadium. I was waiting at the stadium entrance for two hours because they (security) didn't know I was hitting with Rafa. I told them I was hitting with Rafa and they didn't let me in. It was pretty crazy. Toni (Nadal) came down and helped me. Two hours we waited."

Question: Did Rafa offer any advice?

Stefan Kozlov: "He told me I had a good game. I don't remember him giving me any advice. I don't remember, to be honest, but I think he did."

Question: What would you say was the best thing you were able to do against Rafa's game?

Stefan Kozlov: "Really felt comfortable when he was

going high to my backhand. I felt like I could do anything from there. I really like playing spin on the rise. It helped me a lot, I felt like I can really manage his ball."

"He always brings a great energy to the court."

Jamie Murray: "Played him in Indian Wells with Eric Butorac, he played with Feliciano Lopez. The court was packed. He always brings a great energy to the court. It was a lot of fun playing against him. It was tough but fortunately we were able to win, which was cool."

Question: Standout memories of the match?

Jamie Murray: "Just that there was a lot of people there and we played at night. It was a great atmosphere. It was good fun for us to play. It's not always like that."

Question: How were you able to defeat them?

Jamie Murray: "To be honest, I don't really remember much from the match. It was like seven years ago."

Question: Lasting memory of Rafa, on or off court?

Jamie Murray: "He's everything you should wish to be in a tennis player. Any kid that's trying to become a professional tennis player should look to him. Everything that he stands for - pretty classy, stable, he's got a lot of friends on the Tour, all the players respect him for what he's doing on and off court. And he's a good guy."

Murray leads doubles series

2007   Indian Wells   R32   Murray/Burotac vs. Nadal/F. Lopez
L   6-7, 5-7

"Very unbelievable champion."

Jurgen Melzer: "I played him four times. I lost three and beat him once. I mean, he's one of the best competitors in the world. He's never giving you anything. He's not letting you off the hook one point. And that's what made him so strong. He just plays every point like it's match point."

Question: How were you able to turn the tables and beat him?

Jurgen Melzer: "Well, I played a really good match. You have to also say probably in Shanghai is not his favorite surface there. It plays fairly quick. I had a good gameplan that day. I was at my best at that time and I played a great match. You need to be really aggressive and not let him play his game, not let him use his forehands. Yeah, that's how I beat him."

Question: First memory of Nadal?

Jurgen Melzer: "Well, he was playing with his long pants and sleeveless shirts and winning probably everything on clay possible."

Question: A lasting memory of Nadal?

Jurgen Melzer: "Well, of course, it's his superstitions and focus on the court. Best forehand probably in the world in the game. And very unbelievable champion. Very great attitude."

Question: Personal interactions with Nadal?

Jurgen Melzer: "We had a few chats in the locker room. But nothing to put on tape [smiles]."

Nadal leads series 3-1

2008 Beijing Olympics   Hard QF   Nadal 6-0, 6-4

2009 Madrid Masters Clay   R32 Nadal 6-3, 6-1

2010 Roland Garros Clay   SF Nadal 6-2, 6-3, 7-6

2010 Shanghai Masters Hard R16 Melzer 6-1, 3-6, 6-3

"I got injured two days after the match with Rafa."

Jerzy Janowicz: "I remember I did not play my best tennis there. I remember also I got injured two days after the match with Rafa [laughs]."

Question: How?

Jerzy Janowicz: "Actually, I don't know. I just broke my foot. And I think I over-forced my foot and it got broken"

Question: Over-forced it in the match?

Jerzy Janowicz: "I don't know. It's not easy to explain. I don't know, because I was injured for two months with a back disc problem. I played Shanghai and I was out for two months. After this I was practicing really hard. I was able to play three weeks in Stockholm, Valencia and Paris. And right after Paris, I get injured. Just by walking on the street in my hometown (Lodz, Poland)."

Nadal leads series 2-0

2013   Montreal Masters   Hard R16   Nadal   7-6, 6-4

2013   Paris Masters   Hard R16   Nadal 7-5, 6-4

"The first moment he start to play full power."

Yen-Hsun Lu: "I never play Nadal, I only practice with him. First of all, I feel nervous to practice with him. In this time he's number one in the world. Second, I was really impressed from the first moment, first ball he start to play full power. This is what I always keep in my mind. With some other players, from the beginning, they start to get the rhythm first, then slowly, slowly you increase the speed. But Rafa, when he hits the first ball, the second ball you return, he start to play like a real match [smiles]. So this is his style, first of all. Second of all, you can see how serious he is to face each, every ball, even hitting. So this is the mentality I have to say I really respect about him. Of course, everyone's respecting how he fights. How he doesn't give up an inch. So I can see how he's able to be successful. And how strong he can stay in at the top level of tennis."

Question: How did you get the chance to practice with Nadal and where was it?

Yen-Hsun Lu: "Just because of my coach. I practice with him at Wimbledon 2011. But at the time my coach set it up through his coach. Of course we practiced two days in a row. First day, we practice in the morning like a half hour. Second day, even we do warm-up. I mean, it was a great time. It was really for me nice experience. I learned a lot from him from these practices. I just feel a little but unlucky I never played him in a match. I know also I don't really want to play him in the match first round or second round because I know he's very, very tough. And so this is opportunity we get to practice together."

"The guy's doing ten-foot sprints side to side, non-stop."

Hugo Armando: "I played him in Stuttgart. He's the toughest competitor I ever faced. It's just something I've never seen before. It's just everything about him. His energy, just everything. Before walking on the court, the guy's doing ten-foot sprints side to side, just non-stop. It was just unimaginable [smiles]."

Question: Intimidation tactics?

Hugo Armando: "Oh yeah."

Nadal leads series 1-0

2005 Stuttgart Clay R32 Nadal 6-1, 6-2

"I won 7-0 in the tiebreak."

Nicolas Mahut: "The best I ever felt on court was

the tournament Queens 2007, I played Nadal in the quarterfinal. We played almost at night, the crowd was really electric and I played a very good match and I won 7-0 in the tiebreak in second set. So it was almost perfect tennis for me."

Series tied 1-1

2007   Queens Club   Grass QF   Mahut   7-5, 7-6 (0)

2011   US Open   Hard   R64   Nadal   6-2, 6-2, RET

"He was very hungry to play and compete."

Carlos Moya

Question: What is your first memory of Nadal?

Carlos Moya: "Well, meeting him in Stuttgart when he was twelve. He was playing an under-12 tournament and I was playing the Masters 1000 event in Stuttgart ('98). So that was the first time we met."

Question: What was your initial reaction of seeing him play?

Carlos Moya: "We played. We actually played that day and he was twelve and I was twenty-two. I think he was a very great player under twelve, he was very shy off court. But then we saw something different on court. But he was very hungry to play and compete and that's something you could see right away."

(Note: Carlos Moya became the ATP world number one in March of '99.)

Nadal leads series 6-2

2003   Hamburg Masters   Clay R32   Nadal   7-5, 6-4

2003 Umag   Clay   SF   Moya 6-4, 6-4

2005   Montreal Masters   Hard   R64   Nadal   6-3, 6-7, 6-3

2006   Miami Masters   Hard   R64   Moya   2-6, 6-1, 6-1

2007   Roland Garros   Clay   QF   Nadal 6-4, 6-3, 6-0

2008   Chennai   Hard SF   Nadal   6-7, 7-6 (8), 7-6 (1)

2008   Hamburg Masters Clay   SF   Nadal   6-1, 6-3

"I played him when we were fourteen in Slovakia."

Gael Monfils

Question: Your most memorable match with Nadal?

Gael Monfils: "Ah...I don't know...I had one it was cool. I played him when we were maybe fourteen. We play in Slovakia. And it was cool. I lost 63 75 and I liked it."

Question: Why? What happened there?

Gael Monfils: "Because we were young and I know him obviously, not that good. And just the atmosphere was cool."

Nadal leads series 10-2

2005	Monte Carlo Masters	Clay	R64	Nadal	6-3, 6-2
2006	Rome Masters	Clay	SF	Nadal	6-2, 6-2
2008	Paris Masters	Hard	R16	Nadal	6-3, 6-2
2009	Doha	Hard	QF	Monfils	6-4, 6-4
2009	Rotterdam	Hard	SF	Nadal	6-4 6-4
2009	US Open	Hard	R16	Nadal	6-7, 6-3, 6-1 6-3
2010	Madrid Masters	Clay	QF	Nadal	6-1, 6-3
2010	Tokyo	Hard	F	Nadal	6-1, 7-5
2011	Barcelona	Clay	QF	Nadal	6-2, 6-2
2012	Doha	Hard	SF	Monfils	6-3, 6-4
2014	Doha	Hard	F	Nadal	6-1, 6-7, 6-2
2014	Australian Open	Hard	R32	Nadal	6-1, 6-2, 6-3

"You gotta swing hard to fight that thing off."

Taylor Dent: "2010, Cincinnati. For me, personally, I knew our match up was rough on me, especially from the baseline. He just hit the ball so heavy. So I knew that I had to really red line my game. I had to just hit the first shot that I could and rip it as hard as I can. To not get behind in the point. Because once you get behind in the point against Nadal you just don't see it again. He's just got such a big weapon on that forehand side. And he's just so consistent with it. So accurate with it. That it's really, really hard to neutralize that forehand."

Question: Did your gameplan work successfully?

Taylor Dent: "Yeah, in the beginning. I think I got up a break actually. I was up a break in the middle of the set. And you know, anytime you go for a lot, the percentages will catch up with you. And then the percentages caught up with me. And the match ended up being 75 62 or 64 62, something like that."

Question: Is Rafa a hard guy for you to play?

Taylor Dent: "Yeah, I think he's a hard guy for everyone to play [smiles]. His record kind of speaks for itself. One of the things that was interesting was his serve was very deceptive. I think it's very underrated. Is he gonna hit a ton of aces each match?

No. But he has so much spin on it that it's really, really hard to hit a safe return back in play."

Question: Standout memories of being on court in battle with Rafa?

Taylor Dent: "Just the heaviness of the ball. Even in warm-up it's like, Ah, you gotta swing hard just to fight that thing off. Everybody knows he hits the ball big but until you get out there for the match circumstance and feel it for yourself, then you appreciate what it really is."

Question: Before the match, what is Rafa's routine like? I heard he does wind sprints in the locker room?

Taylor Dent: "Yeah, that sounds about right. He gets going in the locker room. He gets it going. He gets a good sweat going and all that sort of stuff. He likes to be physical, get fired up. And so, yeah, it's good. It's interesting. I'm sure he's kind of tweaked his pre-game warmup over the years but it's intense. That's the word for it."

Question: The most intense you've ever seen?

Taylor Dent: "Yeah, I think so."

Nadal leads series 2-0

2010   Miami Masters Hard R64   Nadal 6-4, 6-3

2010   Cincinnati Masters   Hard R32   Nadal 6-2, 7-5

"He plays like a nice person."

Nicolas Massu: "The first memory of Nadal...the best memories. Because he plays like a nice person. And a very good athlete. I think he's one of the best of all times. He's amazing."

Question: Your most memorable match with Rafa?

Nicolas Massu: "I played two matches. One in Toronto, then one in Indian Wells. I lost twice but it was nice to play with one of the best of all times."

Question: Lasting memory of Rafa, on or off court, which captures his essence?

Nicolas Massu: "He has like unbelievable courage, athletic ability, mind, play, everything. So he's one of the best players in the history."

Nadal leads series 2-0

| 2004 | Indian Wells Masters | Hard | R64 | Nadal | 6-3, 1-0 RET |
| 2006 | Toronto Masters | Hard | R64 | Nadal | 6-3, 6-2 |

"Rafa's got too much power for Roger."

Dmitry Tursunov: "I played him in Rotterdam. Actually, the most recent was Rotterdam. It wasn't really a fight with the umpire during the Dimitrov match when I kind of told them that they don't tell Rafa about time violations. It was kind of an inside joke between the two of us because he was doing my match with Rafa in Rotterdam, a few years back. And when he called time, Rafa kept serving and serving and serving and serving. And like when they called time basically, I put in two serves and he put a couple of serves but he just kept going for like another minute. And I was like, sitting. And he told us right before the coin toss, he said warmup ends in five minutes. And then there he is just serving and this guy's just dangling his feet and just smiling. I'm like,

What are you doing?"

"So anyway, it's a couple of years back and I'm
playing Dimitrov and it ends up on You Tube and I'm
getting a lot of crap for it. So I guess that's kind of the
first memory. Rafa is very superstitious in a lot of
ways. So he lets you go first. Just a lot of little things
that he does. That was the first thing. And then I had
to play him in the match. And he's definitely very
threatening, because there's a bit of an aura about it.
He was already going pretty well at the time. So it was
all a little shellshocked. So I had to go to my thoughts,
start the match and try to figure out how to play him.
At first, it was sort of his presence beating me, not
him, so."

Question: What is your most memorable match with
Rafa?

Dmitry Tursunov: "That's tough to say. The few
matches I've played him, I wasn't really able to play
full out. So, recently, I guess I played him in Tokyo.
And I felt like I had a chance there but it just didn't
turn out the way I hoped. He broke me, I broke him
back. We played on a really fast surface in Tokyo,
with balls that I actually liked. So I had a few chances
there but wasn't able, I wasn't in great shape - I had
some niggles that - it's tough to play against him if
you're not a hundred percent, I mean even if you're a
hundred-twenty percent it's tough to play him. I'm
happy to play him one day when I'm in full battle gear.
Then I'll be able to really judge and assess how hard
he is in fact and what I need to improve on."

Question: Is Rafa the toughest guy for you to play?

Dmitry Tursunov: "Not necessarily. I think, for me, it was much tougher to play Davydenko. I never felt like I really had any answers for that guy. It was like he was playing Frogger (a video game) with me...whatever I would come up with, he would be in the right place at the right time. Obviously, Rafa is also very tough to play especially on - I'm not going to talk about playing him on clay because I never played him on clay and I don't want to play him on clay - he plays extremely well when he's ahead. I think he almost plays better when he's ahead. Which is unusual, not a lot of people can do that. Most people start trying to protect the lead, he's actually able to pull away from you. He probably has one of the highest levels of focus in maybe the existance of humankind [smiles]. It's pretty uncanny that he's able to focus so well. He's got a few weird things and hitches. Obviously, the most notorious one is the one with the shorts, without being gory. It's really extremely ridiculous the kind of athlete he is, first of all, he's playing left-handed even though he's a righty. His movement is really light. His attention level is what helps him get so many wins. He doesn't seem to ever crash in his attention span."

Question: You mentioned Nikolay Davydenko and what a tough player he was. He is, I believe, the only player with a winning head to head record vs. Rafa.

Dmitry Tursunov: "I think it also depends on how many times they played and then where they played. Having a winning record against somebody - a lot of times it happens. Maybe I'll play against Guga (Kuerten) and I'll have a winning record. I played him on hard courts at the end of his career. I would rather have a losing record against him and play him maybe twenty times and win eight times, than beat him once and have a winning record. Statistics are kind of a funny thing."

"Yeah I remember (Davydenko) beat (Rafa) in Miami on hard courts. He was playing really well there. If anything, it's much easier to beat Rafa on faster surfaces. Because he's not able to use the surface as much as he's able to use the clay. His balls don't bounce as high off the ground. It's like in Formula One, using racing slicks and running them in the rain and you will spin out of control. Somebody who is set up probably much worse than someone with better tires for the conditions - you're not going to be able to beat that car. Rafa's game is much more suited for clay courts. He's a lot more dominant. He's tough to beat but he's still able to play on faster courts as well. It's a pretty dangerous combination."

Question: Is there a player out there, with a style, like you mentioned Davydenko, who you think might be equipped with a type of style who can match up well with Rafa?

Tursunov: "I think a big server is defintely able to play against him. But, generally, someone who doesn't have to play out points as much against him. So a big server who is also able to maybe take some cuts at his serves. And just kind of sneak in a couple of quick points off the return, off of Rafa's serve. So I would say someone like Del Potro would be able to play well against Rafa. Djokovic is able to neutralize a lot of his spin by taking the ball early, by kind of absorbing that attack that Rafa can generate. And then just sort of able to kind of slingshot it back. But he plays much better positioning against Rafa than anybody else so that's why he's done quite well against him. If anything, Rafa can get thrown off by Djokovic more than anybody else."

"Like Roger gets thrown off by Rafa quite a bit. Because Rafa's got too much power for Roger. He can kind of sit on his backhand a little bit and just start abusing it. But Novak kind of does that too to Rafa. He is able to neutralize his weapons and he knows him so well. A lot of times it's tough for Rafa to come up with something extra. His game patterns are so ingrained. He's not going to serve and volley. And to let Novak just figure it out. He knows how to play him better than anybody else. He's able to use his weapons against Rafa's weaknesses better than anybody else."

Question: Lasting memory of Rafa, on or off court?

Dmitry Tursunov: "Winning six or seven Roland Garros's I guess [smiles] is a lasting memory. But, for me, I try not to get starstruck. You get a little extra pressure playing against the big guys. But the more you play them, the more you realize there are ways to beat them. It's like when you meet an incredibly good looking girl in the beginning. You get star struck. You can't talk. After a while, you get really used to it. It's the same thing. You get used to these guys and then if you're able to play them a lot, you get more and more chances of beating them. It's very hard for me to be in awe of another player - because he's my competitor. Okay, he's a much better competitor, better player, than me at the moment. But what you're asking me is much easier to ask someone who is actually watching him. Oh, this guy is unbelievable. We never try to take that approach psychologically because then you're never going to beat the guy if you're always having it in your head that he's unbeatable."

Question: Any personal interactions with Rafa?

Dmitry Tursunov: "I haven't. Not close friends with Rafa. He's always friendly to everybody. Kind of a guy's guy. He seems like someone you can see yourself going to the bar, having a beer with and talk football with, soccer. But we haven't really been good friends, close friends, kind of acquaintances, I would say co-workers. But from different floors [laughs]."

Nadal leads series 3-0

2008   Rotterdam   Hard   R32   Nadal 6-4, 6-4

2009   Indian Wells Masters   Hard R32   Nadal 6-3, 6-3

2010   Tokyo   Hard   QF   Nadal 6-4, 6-1

Chapter 6:   Coaching Perspectives On Facing Rafa

(Photo By Scoop Malinowski.)

"Although he's a ferocious competitor on the court, off the court he's a nice guy, always in a good mood, always nice to people."

Brian Barker (Coach of James Blake)

Question: What is your first memory of Rafael Nadal?

Brian Barker: "The first time James played him at the US Open, second round. James was coming back from his neck injury. I remember Rafa had beaten Andre Agassi the tournament before in Canada, Super Nine (now called Masters 1000). I knew it was going to be a tough match. When the match started - Rafa obviously hits with a lot of heavy spin, he likes to get the ball up on people. And he generally likes playing one-handers. I thought it would be a really tough match-up for James with Rafa getting the ball up on James' backhandl thought that was really gonna be a problem along with Rafa being better and having more success - he was number two in the world at the time. And then the match started. The court was playing quick. And the crowd was behind James. And the ball was staying low. And then it was obvious after a short period of time it was going to be a good battle and I realized James actually had a chance out there."

Question: You said previously that when Rafa was younger he had trouble at times with big pace to his forehand. Please elaborate.

Brian Barker: "He was number two in the world at the time so obviously he wasn't having a lot of problems. If there was one weakness to his game he didn't like big pace to his forehand and you could get some short balls and create from there. At the time coming in on his backhand he didn't quite have the power and accuracy that he has now on his backhand pass. So James' favorite shot was the inside out forehand and he was able to use his inside out forehand to Rafa's forehand and create some short balls and come in on his backhand. James likes to volley. Yeah, that's where he was able to have success."

Question: James won his first three matches against Rafa.

Brian Barker: "Yes, James won the first three times they played but then I think Rafa won the next three. Unfortunately for James, Rafa became a better player than he was in his earlier years."

Question: Lasting memory or anecdote or Rafa?

Brian Barker: "When I think of Rafa, he's the type of player that you want your students to be on the court. He just plays one point at a time. He doesn't look ahead. Nothing upsets him. Nothing rattles him. He just stays the course, one point, one game at a time. Although he's a ferocious competitor on the court, off the court he's a nice guy, always in a good mood, always nice to people. Always friendly. That's the type of person you hope your students become."

"It was clear what you have to do...but it's tough to do."

Boris Sobkin (Coach of Mikhail Youzhny)

"First memory was Dubai he played against Mischa.
I don't remember which round it was. He played
against Mischa and it was - Mischa was really close to
lose and Rafa was young and finally Mischa managed
it in the final set because Rafa made some stupid
mistakes. And I thought, This kid is really talented and
he will be great. Because he's now young doing
stupid things. It will go and he will be really great.
That's my first memory of him."

Question: Is Rafa one of the hardest guys to coach
Mischa to play against?

Boris Sobkin: "No, no, no, no, no, no. It wasn't.
Because, honestly, honestly, it was tough, no I don't
think so.   With Rafa it's...how to say it exactly...Rafa
is really great player but against him it was clear how
to play. But the problem was to do it. It was clear what
you have to do but it was tough to do. That was the
problem. And I think, honestly, me with Mischa, found
the way how to play against Rafa because Mischa
won some good matches against him. But it's always
tough. Sometimes you know what to do but it's tough
to do."

Question: I vividly remember watching one of
Mischa's best matches ever, it was against Rafa on
Armstrong at US Open, late afternoon, close third set
and Mischa was down triple set point, love-40, and he
came back and won the game and then forced a
crucial third set tiebreak, also coming from behind in
that and winning that, then winning the fourth set to

win the match. Rafa had a confused, shell-shocked look on his face after the third set that we rarely see.

Boris Sobkin: "It was great. Mischa played good. He played smart. He was in good mood, it was quarterfinal. It was good match. But there was also some other good matches."

Question: Youzhny was amazing that day. You mean that wasn't the best match he ever played?

Boris Sobkin: "No, I don't think. It's tough to say the best match or not the best match. The problem is comparing, this match was good. Mischa played good to get to the semifinal here (US Open). But there was also good match he played first against him in Chennai, he beat Rafa 61 60, something like this. But Rafa was tired, he played the semifinal before against Moya for four hours. Moya prepared him really good [smiles] for this match. Rafa is a great player, honestly. I like him so much. And I like the way how he communicates with Toni. He's really nice person, really one of the nicest persons in the Tour, if not to say the nicest one. So he is great."

Question: Which are the tactics that work against Rafa, which you mentioned earlier?

Boris Sobkin: "No, I don't want to tell, sorry [smiles]."

Question: Lasting memory of Rafa, on or off court?

Boris Sobkin: "He is really a good, educated kid, he is a really polite guy. Toni is really polite and great person. I think smart."

Question: You obviously know Uncle Toni. What is it that's so special about him?

Boris Sobkin: "Toni is really smart. He understands what to say, what to do, not to do.   He is not only coach, he is teacher in life, also, this is also very important. Because tennis is not the whole life. And Toni teaches him not only play tennis but how to behave, how to respect people. It's really important."

Question: What would you say is your most memorable match of Rafa?

Boris Sobkin: "Mischa, for sure, here years ago (2006). This for sure."

Question: Why this match?

Boris Sobkin: "Because Mischa played good. It was quarterfinal. Mischa reached (his first major) quarterfinal. It was tough to reach quarterfinal. It was really tough along way to quarterfinal.   And finally he reached semifinal, of course, this is most memorable."

Question: Mischa's best performance?

Boris Sobkin: "Mischa did some great matches in Davis Cup. Against France. Davis Cup semifinal 2006 againsts James Blake in Moscow. It was key match actually. He had some great matches here. Quarterfinal here against Wawrinka. They both played maybe not great but Mischa was fighting like hell. Finally he won that match. He was down two to one by sets."

Question: Who is the hardest guy for Mischa to play against?

Boris Sobkin: "Federer, for sure. Because he never won against him [laughs]. In singles, one he beat Roger in junior doubles. Just one match."

'I don't want to be negative already but I could really get embarrassed out there.'

Billy Heiser (Coach of Tim Smyczek)

Question: You were a part of one of the most memorable matches of the 2015 Australian Open, coaching Tim Smyczek vs. Rafael Nadal, five set match. What are some of your stand-out memories of this match?

Billy Heiser: "It was obviously very memorable for Tim and I. Hopefully it was memorable for the fans and they got a good match to watch early in the tournament. Any time you get to play against one of the greatest players of all time on one of the biggest courts of all time, it's gonna be special. So that's kind of the attitude that Tim went out there with, try and control the things he could control, and have fun. If he took care of the things we talked about, then he'd have a shot."

Question: It was the first time Tim played Rafa or even was on court with Rafa right? What were the expectations?

Billy Heiser: "Right. First time he ever hit with Rafa or played Rafa. When he won his first round, I remember he asked me who he played and I said, 'Rafa.' And the first thing he told me was, 'I don't want to be negative already but I could really get embarrassed out there.' And I just kinda looked at him and said, 'Yeah, you could.' And then we talked about it for a while. Really talked about controlling the things he could control and focus on the things he had control of. We agreed, if he did that, he'd put himself in a position to be competitive and, possibly, win the match. So that's really what he went out there trying to do."

Question: What tactics were successful?

Billy Heiser: "Well, I don't know how much I want to go in-depth about tactics playing against another player. But I thought Tim served really smart and played really smart from the back of the court. And I think that helped him to have a clear idea of what he was trying to do out there."

Question: Did anything surprise you about the match?

Billy Heiser: "Not really. You always now what you're gonna get with Rafa. Not surprising but what always impresses me with Nadal is how professional he is in terms of his routines and rituals and all the things that he does during a match. The guy is perfect out there in terms of attitude and effort. It doesn't get any better than watching him struggle as much as he was physically and yet there's no drama. He's not letting the world know that he's struggling. He's going about his business trying to fight as tough as he can to win that match. And then you see the reaction from him...to get through that match. And he's on his knees. It's really cool to see someone who has the amount of money he has, the amount of Grand Slam titles he's won, the amount of matches he's won, and yet fighting through and battling through the second round of a major means that much to him. It was really cool to see."

Question: Describe the mindset of Tim after the match?

Billy Heiser: "He was fine. We had a nice laugh. A lot of his guys from the tennis community that we know close from growing up, came out to watch and were in his box. A couple of the young Americans were in his box. We had a good group of guys that he's friends with. So, after, I went into the players lounge and grabbed about eight doughnuts from the cafeteria. We all just sat in the locker room and just laughed and had a good time and reminiscing about the match, the experience. He wasn't too down. Obviously he felt he could win the match and he was disappointed he didn't. But he's always a pretty big picture kind of guy. I think he saw the big picture pretty quickly."

Question: The match featured the famous sportsmanship moment in the final set when Tim gave Rafa the serve again after the loud heckler disrupted Rafa's serve. Your comments?

Billy Heiser: "Honestly, it's probably being blown up a little bit and made into too much of a deal. Anyone who knows Tim, knows it's not uncommon from him. I don't think it's uncommon from a lot of guys. I've seen a lot of guys who have done that in that situation. Maybe watching on TV it didn't seem that fan yelled that loud or was that big of a deal. But it was no doubt a distraction to Rafa. And just the right thing to do, regardless of the score. It's one thing that Tim can go on the court and walk off the court with his character. He's not going to let any amount of success define what kind of person he is. He is just going to do the right thing."

Question: Lasting impressions of Rafael Nadal?

Billy Heiser: "Someone for every kid that wants to be a professional tennis player to watch. There is no one in the world who does the little things better than him. Like all the things I feel that make up a tennis player, he does perfectly."

Chapter 7:   Nadal's 2005 ATP Match Record

(Photo By Henk Abbink.)

Rafael Nadal was named the ATP's Most Improved Player of the Year in 2005, his second full season on the ATP World Tour, in which he won the French Open and eleven overall singles titles (a teenage record) and achieved the No. 2 singles ranking.

ATP Masters Series Madrid, Spain; 17.10.2005; SU; Indoor: Hard; Draw: 48

Round Opponent Ranking Score

R64 Bye   N/A   W

R32 Victor Hanescu (ROU)   42   W 7-6(5), 6-3

R16 Tommy Robredo (ESP)   17   W 6-2, 6-4

Q Radek Stepanek (CZE)   14   W 7-6(9), 6-4

S Robby Ginepri (USA)   21   W 7-5, 7-6(1)

W Ivan Ljubicic (CRO)   12   W 3-6, 2-6, 6-3, 6-4, 7-6(3)

This Event Points: 500, ATP Ranking: 2, Prize Money: $450,000

ITA vs. ESP WG PO, Torre Del Greco, Ita; 23.09.2005; DAVIS CUP; Outdoor: Clay;

RR Daniele Bracciali (ITA)   92   W 6-3, 6-2, 6-1

RR Andreas Seppi (ITA)   78   W 6-1, 6-2, 5-7, 6-4

ATP Ranking: 2

Beijing, China; 12.09.2005; WS; Outdoor: Hard; Draw: 32

R32 Jimmy Wang (TPE)   100   W 6-2, 6-4

R16 Justin Gimelstob (USA)   95   W 5-7, 6-4, 6-4

Q Peter Wessels (NED)   115   W 7-6(3), 6-2

S Juan Carlos Ferrero (ESP)   23   W 6-4, 6-4

W Guillermo Coria (ARG)   8   W 5-7, 6-1, 6-2

This Event Points: 175, ATP Ranking: 2, Prize Money: $69,200

US Open, NY, U.S.A.; 29.08.2005; GS; Outdoor: Hard; Draw: 128

R128 Bobby Reynolds (USA)   132   W 6-3, 6-3, 6-4

R64 Scoville Jenkins (USA)   352   W 6-4, 7-5, 6-4

R32 James Blake (USA)   49   L 4-6, 6-4, 3-6, 1-6

This Event Points: 75, ATP Ranking: 2, Prize Money: $50,000

ATP Masters Series Cincinnati, Ohio, USA; 15.08.2005; SU; Outdoor: Hard; Draw: 64

R64 Tomas Berdych (CZE)   36   L 7-6(4), 2-6, 6-7(3)

This Event Points: 5, ATP Ranking: 2, Prize Money: $7,500

ATP Masters Series Canada, Montreal, Canada; 08.08.2005; SU; Outdoor: Hard; Draw: 64

R64 Carlos Moya (ESP)   32   W 6-3, 6-7(0), 6-3

R32 Ricardo Mello (BRA)   56   W 6-1, 6-2

R16 Sebastien Grosjean (FRA)   34   W 6-4, 6-4

Q Mariano Puerta (ARG)   11   W 6-3, 6-1

S Paul-Henri Mathieu (FRA)   63   W 6-4, 7-5

W Andre Agassi (USA)   7   W 6-3, 4-6, 6-2

This Event Points: 500, ATP Ranking: 2, Prize Money: $400,000

Stuttgart, Germany; 18.07.2005; CS; Outdoor: Clay; Draw: 48

R64 Bye   N/A   W

R32 Hugo Armando (USA)   167   W 6-1, 6-2

R16 Fernando Verdasco (ESP)   58   W 6-3, 6-2

Q Tomas Zib (CZE)   57   W 6-2, 6-1

S Jarkko Nieminen (FIN)   66   W 6-2, 7-5

W Gaston Gaudio (ARG)   13   W 6-3, 6-3, 6-4

This Event Points: 250, ATP Ranking: 3, Prize Money: $122,850

Bastad, Sweden; 04.07.2005; WS; Outdoor: Clay; Draw: 32

R32 Juan Monaco (ARG)   66   W 6-1, 6-1

R16 Alberto Martin (ESP)   50   W 6-2, 6-4

Q Juan Carlos Ferrero (ESP)   31   W 6-3, 6-3

S Tommy Robredo (ESP)   20   W 6-3, 6-3

W Tomas Berdych (CZE)   42   W 2-6, 6-2, 6-4

This Event Points: 175, ATP Ranking: 3, Prize Money: $52,000

Wimbledon, England; 20.06.2005; GS; Outdoor: Grass; Draw: 128

R128 Vincent Spadea (USA)   39   W 6-4, 6-3, 6-0

R64 Gilles Muller (LUX)   69   L 4-6, 6-4, 3-6, 4-6

This Event Points: 35, ATP Ranking: 3, Prize Money: $28,255

Halle, Germany; 06.06.2005; WS; Outdoor: Grass; Draw: 32

R32 Alexander Waske (GER)   147   L 6-4, 5-7, 3-6

This Event Points: 5, ATP Ranking: 3, Prize Money: $7,950

Roland Garros, France; 23.05.2005; GS; Outdoor: Clay; Draw: 128

R128 Lars Burgsmuller (GER)   96   W 6-1, 7-6(4), 6-1

R64 Xavier Malisse (BEL)   46   W 6-2, 6-2, 6-4

R32 Richard Gasquet (FRA)   31   W 6-4, 6-3, 6-2

R16 Sebastien Grosjean (FRA)   24   W 6-4, 3-6, 6-0, 6-3

Q David Ferrer (ESP)   21   W 7-5, 6-2, 6-0

S Roger Federer (SUI)   1   W 6-3, 4-6, 6-4, 6-3

W Mariano Puerta (ARG)   37   W 6-7(6), 6-3, 6-1, 7-5

This Event Points: 1,000, ATP Ranking: 5, Prize Money: $1,103,960

ATP Masters Series Rome, Italy; 02.05.2005; SU; Outdoor: Clay; Draw: 64

R64 Mikhail Youzhny (RUS)   26   W 6-0, 6-2

R32 Victor Hanescu (ROU)   85   W 6-1, 6-1

R16 Guillermo Canas (ARG)   13   W 6-3, 6-1

Q Radek Stepanek (CZE)   17   W 5-7, 6-1, 6-1

S David Ferrer (ESP)   25   W 4-6, 6-4, 7-5

W Guillermo Coria (ARG)   11   W 6-4, 3-6, 6-3, 4-6, 7-6(6)

This Event Points: 500, ATP Ranking: 7, Prize Money: $400,000

Barcelona, Spain; 18.04.2005; CS; Outdoor: Clay; Draw: 56

R64 Bye   N/A   W

R32 Gilles Muller (LUX)   64   W 6-0, 6-2

R16 Dominik Hrbaty (SVK)   25   W 6-1, 6-2

Q Agustin Calleri (ARG)   99   W 6-2, 3-0 RET

S Radek Stepanek (CZE)   22   W 7-5, 6-2

W Juan Carlos Ferrero (ESP)   58   W 6-1, 7-6(4), 6-3

This Event Points: 300, ATP Ranking: 11, Prize Money:

$153,000

ATP Masters Series Monte Carlo, Monaco; 11.04.2005; SU; Outdoor: Clay; Draw: 64

R64 Gael Monfils (FRA)   106   W 6-3, 6-2

R32 Xavier Malisse (BEL)   38   W 6-0, 6-3

R16 Olivier Rochus (BEL)   42   W 6-1, 6-2

Q Gaston Gaudio (ARG)   6   W 6-3, 6-0

S Richard Gasquet (FRA)   101   W 6-7(6), 6-4, 6-3

W Guillermo Coria (ARG)   9   W 6-3, 6-1, 0-6, 7-5

This Event Points: 500, ATP Ranking: 17, Prize Money: $400,000

Valencia, Spain; 04.04.2005; WS; Outdoor: Clay; Draw: 32

R32 Juan C. Ferrero (ESP)   68   W 6-2, 6-1

R16 Guillermo Garcia-Lopez (ESP)   80   W 6-1, 6-4

Q Igor Andreev (RUS)   47   L 5-7, 2-6

This Event Points: 40, ATP Ranking: 17, Prize Money: $11,125

ATP Masters Series Miami, FL, U.S.A.; 21.03.2005; SU; Outdoor: Hard; Draw: 96

R128 Bye N/A W

R64 Rainer Schuettler (GER)   39   W 6-4, 7-6(5)

R32 Fernando Verdasco (ESP)   45   W 6-2, 6-2

R16 Ivan Ljubicic (CRO)   14   W 6-4, 6-7(5), 6-3

Q Thomas Johansson (SWE)   27   W 6-2, 6-4

S David Ferrer (ESP)   44   W 6-4, 6-3

F Roger Federer (SUI)   1   L 6-2, 7-6(4), 6-7(5), 3-6, 1-6

This Event Points: 350, ATP Ranking: 31, Prize Money: $266,675

Acapulco, Mexico; 21.02.2005; CS; Outdoor: Clay; Draw: 32

R32 Alex Calatrava (ESP)   81   W 6-4, 6-4

R16 Santiago Ventura (ESP)   77   W 7-6(0), 6-2

Q Guillermo Canas (ARG)   12   W 7-5, 6-3

S Mariano Puerta (ARG)   74   W 6-4, 6-1

W Albert Montanes (ESP)   95   W 6-1, 6-0

This Event Points: 250, ATP Ranking: 39, Prize Money: $118,750

Costa Do Sauipe, Brazil; 14.02.2005; WS; Outdoor: Clay; Draw: 32

R32 Jose Acasuso (ARG)   55   W 7-6(1), 6-3

R16 Alex Calatrava (ESP)   86   W 6-3, 6-3

Q Agustin Calleri (ARG)   60   W 6-2, 6-7(5), 6-4

S Ricardo Mello (BRA)   56   W 2-6, 6-2, 6-4

W Alberto Martin (ESP)   61   W 6-0, 6-7(2), 6-1

This Event Points: 175, ATP Ranking: 48, Prize Money: $52,000

Buenos Aires, Argentina; 07.02.2005; WS; Outdoor: Clay; Draw: 32

R32 Agustin Calleri (ARG)   61   W 7-6(2), 6-3

R16 Potito Starace (ITA)   66   W 6-1, 6-3

Q Gaston Gaudio (ARG)   8   L 6-0, 0-6, 1-6

This Event Points: 40, ATP Ranking: 48, Prize Money: $10,600

Australian Open, Australia; 17.01.2005; GS; Outdoor: Hard; Draw: 128

R128 Julien Benneteau (FRA)   65   W 6-0, 6-4, 6-2

R64 Mikhail Youzhny (RUS)   15   W 6-1, 4-6, 4-6, 7-5, 6-3

R32 Bobby Reynolds (USA)   283   W 6-1, 6-1, 6-3

R16 Lleyton Hewitt (AUS)   3   L 5-7, 6-3, 6-1, 6-7(3), 2-6

This Event Points: 150, ATP Ranking: 56, Prize Money: $57,312

Auckland, New Zealand; 10.01.2005; WS; Outdoor: Hard; Draw: 32

R32 Dominik Hrbaty (SVK)   20   L 3-6 RET

This Event Points: 5, ATP Ranking: 50, Prize Money: $4,150

Doha, Qatar; 03.01.2005; WS; Outdoor: Hard; Draw: 32

R32 Mikhail Youzhny (RUS)   16   W 6-3, 7-6(3)

R16 Fernando Verdasco (ESP)   36   W 6-2, 6-4

Q Ivan Ljubicic (CRO)   22   L 2-6, 7-6(3), 3-6

This Event Points: 60, ATP Ranking: 51, Prize Money: $29,000

SOURCE: ATPWorldTour.com

August 14, 2005

Rafael Nadal Interview after his Montreal Masters final win vs. Andre Agassi in three sets.

THE MODERATOR: Rafa wins his ATP best ninth tournament title of the season. Also the first teenager to win nine titles in a season since Mats Wilander won nine back in 1983. It was also his third ATP Masters

Series title this season. Questions for Rafa.

Q. How important is it to win your first hard court tournament?

RAFAEL NADAL: Yeah, it's very important. I know I can play good in hard because I have some good scores this year. But for me win here is very, very nice. I get confidence now. I hope play the same level the next weeks because that's very good for the confidence for the US Open especially. No, I am very happy because I say before come here my goal is win any tournament in hard this year. I have that in the first, no?

Q. If you can win a Masters on hard, can you win a Grand Slam on hard?

RAFAEL NADAL: I don't like speak about that because I know if I am playing good, I have a little bit chance. But I always say, I always want to think about the first round. If I win the first round, the second round. If I win the second, the third. If I stay in one semifinal of Grand Slam, I can think about the victories. But for arrive to a semifinal, this round is very large, so I need won a lot of matches. Of course, my goal for any year is win any tournament, any Grand Slam, in hard, too, no? But I always want to say I only hope -- I only think about the first rounds normally.

Q. Can you talk about playing against Agassi?

RAFAEL NADAL: Yes, today it was a very tough match for me. I think in the first set I have the control of the situation. I have very good feelings in the third because Andre is -- (switching to Spanish).

ATP: Rafa felt comfortable because Andre was not really putting too much pressure on him, and he was allowing him to play his game.

RAFAEL NADAL: But after, with the stop, with the rain stop, he come back and he change all the strategy in the game, no? He put his backhand on my backhand always. In the first set, he come to the backhand with my forehand, that's better for me. After he change, he put the backhand in my backhand, and I have problem. He play unbelievable aggressive. He surprise me in the second set. I can win the first four game games, but 5-4, he play a good game and he have break me and the second set is for him. In the third set, he begin with a lot of confidence. I am watching the match in court, and I say with me, "Is very difficult because he's playing with a lot of confidence. He's playing very tough, a lot of aggressive, and that's very difficult for me. I think I need to play a little more aggressive for trying, for try the victory. I do that. I play more aggressive, and that's -- for that reason I think I can change the situation.

Q. Were you having trouble with your shoes or with your feet?

RAFAEL NADAL: No, the shoes is totally broke.

Q. Broke?

RAFAEL NADAL: Yeah, total. When I play in these courts, I have always the same way. I broke the shoes always.

Q. When you say it's broken, the soles were worn down, the bottoms?

ATP: Yeah, that's pretty much it. The insole just broke and ripped out.

Q. Would you say after losing the second set, the win was as much mental as physical for you because you'd never won on hard before?

RAFAEL NADAL: I always think all is mental because you have some points, some important points. Always in every match, you have important points. If you stay comfortable, if you stay tough mentally, you can do always these points. If you am feel good in these moments, if you think, "I don't going to win the point," normally you going to lose. So you need think about always, "I must do that for try, for try the victory." After you think that for trying that, no? I think I need play more aggressive and for victory I know I need play more aggressive.

Q. Did you feel the crowd as much behind you during the final as it was in the course of the week or did you feel it was more in favor of Andre?

RAFAEL NADAL: No, of course, the public stay with Andre. Is normal. I understand for sure because he play here all times, a lot of times. He's one of the best in the history. He's an idol in all sides. I know that. But every time in this week, the public support me a lot. And today support me, but normally a little bit more Andre, no (smiling)?

Q. How much do you think age played a part in your win, the difference in your age? You're 19; he's 35.

RAFAEL NADAL: I don't know. I don't know.

Q. You've played so much this year, you won so much this year, do you ever get mentally tired?

RAFAEL NADAL: I was tired after Rome, when I won in Rome, when I won the final in five hours against Coria, I was tired. After Roland Garros, when I won Roland Garros, a little bit down because I finish the first season of the year, and I play unbelievable. But after I don't play -- I play very well in Wimbledon the first round, and second round I don't feel a lot of concentration, I don't feel good. After that, I come back very well, no? I have one week stop, Bastad, one week stop, Stuttgart, one week and four days stop, and here. In the last month, I have tournament, stop, tournament, stop. Now I have tournament, tournament, stop (smiling). I feel good. I have a good feelings. I feel tough mentally. That's the most important thing, because if I feel tough mentally, I feel good physically, I feel good with the forehand, good with the backhand. If I don't feel good like here (pointing to his head), always is difficult. Always is difficult.

Q. You're in the midst of the greatest season for a teenager since Mats Wilander in 1983, the best ever. Do you go, Wow, that's me?

RAFAEL NADAL: Sorry, but I don't think about that. I don't like think about that because I want to say always the same. I always want to think about the next weeks. I know I am very happy because I win three Masters Series, one Grand Slam, five tournaments. That's unbelievable for me. But I can't think about that now. I want to think about that when I finish the year. Now I finish my goals, and I need improve every day for the next tournaments and for the next years. I can't think I playing unbelievable. I only want to think about improve and the next goals.

Rafael Nadal photos by Henk Abbink

Mark "Scoop" Malinowski, of Teaneck, NJ and Bradenton, FL, has been writing about tennis since 1992 for such outlets as Tennis Magazine, Tennis Week magazine, ATPWorldTour.com, Totally Tennis, Florida Tennis, Australian Tennis, Ace Magazine, New York Tennis, Tennis-prose.com. This is his fourth tennis book (*Marcelo Rios: The Man We Barely Knew, Facing Federer, Facing Hewitt.*) He is currently working on *Facing McEnroe,* and *Facing Serena.*

©Henk Abbink

Made in the USA
Middletown, DE
17 May 2021